BOOKS AVAILABLE

Excel 95 explained

by

N. Kantaris
and
P.R.M. Oliver

BERNARD BABANI (publishing) LTD.
THE GRAMPIANS
SHEPHERDS BUSH ROAD
LONDON W6 7NF
ENGLAND

PLEASE NOTE

Although every care has been taken with the production of this book to ensure that any projects, designs, modifications and/or programs, etc., contained herewith, operate in a correct and safe manner and also that any components specified are normally available in Great Britain, the Publishers and Author(s) do not accept responsibility in any way for the failure (including fault in design) of any project, design, modification or program to work correctly or to cause damage to any equipment that it may be connected to or used in conjunction with, or in respect of any other damage or injury that may be so caused, nor do the Publishers accept responsibility in any way for the failure to obtain specified components.

Notice is also given that if equipment that is still under warranty is modified in any way or used or connected with home-built equipment then that warranty may be void.

© 1996 BERNARD BABANI (publishing) LTD

First Published - October 1996

British Library Cataloguing in Publication Data:

A catalogue record for this book is available from the
British Library

ISBN 0 85934 407 X

Cover Design by Gregor Arthur
Cover illustration by Adam Willis
Printed and Bound in Great Britain by Cox & Wyman Ltd, Reading

ABOUT THIS BOOK

Excel 95 explained has been written for those who want to get to grips with the latest 3-dimensional spreadsheet for Windows 95 (version 7) from Microsoft in the fastest possible time. The material in this book is presented on the 'what you need to know first, appears first' basis, although the underlying structure is such that you don't have to start at the beginning and go right through to the end. The more experienced user can start from any section, as they have been designed to be self contained.

No previous knowledge is assumed, but the book does not describe how to set up your computer hardware, or how to install and use Windows 95. If you need to know more about the Windows environment, then we suggest you select an appropriate level book for your needs from the 'Books Available' list - the books are graduated in complexity with the less demanding *One step at a time* series, to the more detailed *Explained* series. They are all published by BERNARD BABANI (publishing) Ltd.

Microsoft Excel for Windows 95 is a very powerful spreadsheet package that has the ability to work 3-dimensionally with both multiple worksheets and files. It is operated by selecting commands from drop-down menus, by using buttons, or by writing 'macros' to chain together menu commands. Each method of accessing the package is discussed separately, but the emphasis is mostly in the area of menu-driven and button clicking command selection. Working under the Windows 95 environment, gives the package an excellent WYSIWYG appearance which, in turn, allows for the production of highly professional quality printed material.

Overleaf, we list the major enhancements found in Microsoft Excel Version 7 for Windows 95 over Version 5. These are:

- The inclusion of the TipWizard which allows you to learn shortcuts for the way you work.

- The ability to display ToolTips to see button names.

- The ability to enter and edit data directly in a cell or in the formula bar, and check your spelling.

- The ability to manage data simply by treating all files as workbooks.

- The inclusion of the Find File command to search for a workbook, even if its name is not known.

- The inclusion of the Format Painter button to quickly copy formats between cells and between objects.

- The ability to create named ranges in the Name box on the formula bar.

- The ability to create custom AutoFill series and automatically create grand totals with AutoSum.

- The ability to create 3-D formulae and 3-D names for powerful workbook models.

- The inclusion of the interactive Function Wizard to create formulae with worksheet functions.

- The ability to drag data directly onto a chart to add a data series or data points, and add trendlines and error bars to your data series.

- The ability to draw graphic objects directly on charts and to position objects, such as titles, anywhere you want them.

- The ability to sort data by using column labels from a list and the creation of custom sort orders, such as High, Med, and Low.

- The ability to access external databases with Microsoft Query and the use of the interactive

PivotTable Wizard to cross-tabulate and summarise data from an existing list or table.

- The inclusion of the Scenario Manager to create, manage, and track changes to scenarios.

- The ability to use or customise any of the built-in toolbars, or create your own.

- The ability to use autotemplates to create new default workbooks and sheets.

- The inclusion of Visual Basic Programming System to create custom solutions in Microsoft Excel.

- The ability to display the precedent, dependent, and error tracers directly on your worksheet to locate problems in formulae.

- The inclusion of Object Linking and Embedding (OLE) allows you to link objects without leaving Microsoft Excel.

In addition to the above new features, Microsoft Excel Version 7 supports all the functionality built into Version 5, such as:

- Solving What-if problems by seeking a value that solves a formula.

- Using the Solver to analyse multiple-variable problems.

- Using the Data Analysis Tool to make statistical or engineering analysis easier.

In Microsoft Excel 7, there are two ways in which you can learn about and use the various worksheet functions. These are:

- Online Help, which includes complete worksheet function descriptions - search Help for 'worksheet functions'.

- The Function Wizard, which includes descriptions of all worksheet functions. It can be used to select a function, assemble the arguments correctly, and insert it into your formula.

Most features of the package (old and new) will be discussed using simple examples that the user is encouraged to type in, save, and modify as more advanced features are introduced. This provides the new user with a set of examples that aim to help with the learning of the most commonly used features of the package, and should help to provide the confidence needed to tackle some of the more advanced features of the package later.

Although the book is intended as a supplement to the documentation that comes with the package, at the back of the book, all the Excel functions are listed so that it is self contained and can be used as a reference long after you become an expert in the use of the program.

ABOUT THE AUTHORS

Noel Kantaris graduated in Electrical Engineering at Bristol University and after spending three years in the Electronics Industry in London, took up a Tutorship in Physics at the University of Queensland. Research interests in Ionospheric Physics, led to the degrees of M.E. in Electronics and Ph.D. in Physics. On return to the UK, he took up a Post-Doctoral Research Fellowship in Radio Physics at the University of Leicester, and then in 1973 a lecturing position in Engineering at the Camborne School of Mines, Cornwall, (part of Exeter University), where since 1978 he has also assumed the responsibility for the Computing Department.

Phil Oliver graduated in Mining Engineering at Camborne School of Mines in 1967 and since then has specialised in most aspects of surface mining technology, with a particular emphasis on computer related techniques. He has worked in Guyana, Canada, several Middle Eastern countries, South Africa and the United Kingdom, on such diverse projects as: the planning and management of bauxite, iron, gold and coal mines; rock excavation contracting in the UK; international mining equipment sales and technical back up and international mine consulting for a major mining house in South Africa. In 1988 he took up a lecturing position at Camborne School of Mines (part of Exeter University) in Surface Mining and Management.

ACKNOWLEDGEMENTS

We would like to thank the staff of Text 100 Limited for providing the software programs on which this work was based. We would also like to thank colleagues at the Camborne School of Mines for the helpful tips and suggestions which assisted us in the writing of this book.

TRADEMARKS

CONTENTS

1. INTRODUCTION

Microsoft Excel 95 is a powerful and versatile software package which has proved its usefulness, not only in the business world, but also within the scientific and engineering spheres. The program's power lies in its ability to emulate everything that can be done by the use of pencil, paper and a calculator. It is an 'electronic spreadsheet' or simply a 'spreadsheet', and its power is derived from the power of the computer it is running on, and the flexibility and accuracy with which it can deal with the solution of the various applications it is programmed to manage. These can vary from budgeting and forecasting to the solution of complex scientific and engineering problems.

Microsoft Excel 7 for Windows 95 is backwards compatible to spreadsheets built up on previous versions of Excel or, indeed, to other spreadsheets, such as Lotus 1-2-3, Quattro Pro, and Microsoft Works, which can easily be made to run on this version of Excel. Once you have overcome the first hurdle and started to use Excel 95, you will find it both intuitive and an easy program to produce the type of work output you would not have dreamt possible.

Excel, in common with all other MS Office 95 applications, makes use of IntelliSense, which anticipates what you want to do and produces the correct result. For example, AutoCorrect and Auto-Format can, when activated, correct common spelling mistakes and format an entire workbook automatically. Other Wizards can help you with everyday tasks and/or make complex tasks easier to manage.

With OfficeLinks and OLE (Object Linking and Embedding), you can move and share information seamlessly between MS Office 95 applications by simply dragging information from one application to another. Finally, Microsoft Visual Basic for Applications, gives you a powerful and flexible development platform for creating custom solutions.

Hardware Requirements

If Microsoft Word is already installed on your computer, you can safely skip the rest of this chapter.

To install and run Excel 95 successfully, you need an IBM compatible Intel's 80386sx (or higher) processor. We recommend a minimum processor speed of 33 megahertz (MHz). In addition, you need the following:

- Windows 95, Windows NT or Windows NT Advanced Server version.

- Random access memory (RAM): 4MB; 8MB recommended when running more than one MS Office program.

- Hard disc space available for MS Excel 95: 13.6MB for Excel and 3 MB for converters, filters, and data access tools.

- Video adapter: VGA or higher resolution. If you are embedding colour pictures, you will need a 256-colour video adapter.

- Pointing device: Microsoft Mouse or compatible.

Realistically, to run Microsoft Excel for Windows 95 with reasonable sized applications, you will need a 486 or a Pentium PC with at least 8MB of RAM. To run Microsoft Excel 95 from a network, you must also have a network compatible with your Windows operating environment.

Although it is possible to operate from the keyboard alone, the availability of a mouse is a must if you are going to benefit from the program's features and from Window's Graphical User Interface (GUI). After all, pointing and clicking at an option on the screen, is a lot easier than having to learn several different key combinations. So, if you can, install a mouse.

New Features

Some of the major enhancements Microsoft Excel 95 has over earlier releases of the package include:

- The new Answer Wizard which uses IntelliSense to determine the type of help you need.

- The AutoCalculate facility which produces the sum of a selected range automatically and displays it on the Status bar at the bottom of the screen.

- The AutoComplete facility which allows you to type the first few letters of an entry in a cell, then use the right-mouse button to complete the entry from a list, based on the entries you have already made in that column.

- The AutoCorrect facility which when selected, can correct common mistakes as you type.

- The improved drag-and-drop editing facility which can be used to easily move or copy selected ranges between worksheets and workbooks.

- The ability to add explanatory information, called cell tips, to individual worksheet cells.

- The ability to analyse sales or market research data by geographical regions by arranging your data in columns on a worksheet.

- The ability to find, open, or manage documents in the same way as in all the other MS Office applications.

- The ability to create shared lists so that several users can work with the same data.

Other improved features deal with formatting numbers, charts, organising data, and retrieving and analysing data from lists and tables.

Installing Excel

Installing Excel on your computer's hard disc is made very easy with the use of the SETUP program, which even configures Excel automatically to take advantage of the computer's hardware.

If you are installing from floppy discs, insert the first SETUP disc (Disc 1) in the A: drive, or if you are installing from a CD-ROM, insert the CD in the CD-ROM drive. If you are installing from a network drive, make a note of the drive letter because you will need it later. Then do the following:

- Click the **Start** button on the Windows 95 Taskbar and select **Settings**, **Control Panel**.

- On the displayed Control Panel window, double-click the Add/Remove Programs icon, shown here.

- On the Add/Remove Programs Properties dialogue box, click the Install/Uninstall tab and press the **Install** button.

- SETUP will scan your disc for already installed parts of Microsoft Office and will advise you as to the folder in which you should install Excel. This will most likely be **Msoffice** - we suggest you accept all the default options.

- Follow the SETUP instructions on the screen, until the installation of Excel program files starts. When a new disc is required (if you are installing from floppy discs), SETUP will inform you by displaying an appropriate dialogue box.

When all discs have been read, the SETUP program will modify your system files automatically so that you can start Excel easily by creating and displaying a new entry in the **Start**, **Programs** cascade menu, with the icon shown here. Clicking this menu entry will start Microsoft Excel.

4

The Office Shortcut Bar:

If you have MS-Office installed, SETUP also adds Excel to the Microsoft Shortcut Bar. This provides a convenient way to work with your documents and the Office applications (including Microsoft Excel) by complementing the Windows 95 **Start** menu.

The various icons on the Shortcut Bar, shown below, have the following function:

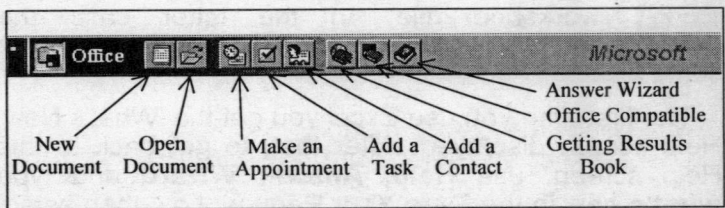

The Start a New Document button: Allows you to select in the displayed dialogue box the tab containing the type of document you want to work with. Double-clicking the type of document or template you want, automatically loads the appropriate application.

The Open a Document button: Allows you to work with an existing document. Opening a document, first starts the application originally used to create it.

The Schedule buttons: Allow you to schedule an appointment, or a task, and add a contact name.

Getting Results Book button: Provides you with suggestions on how to work efficiently with the Microsoft Office applications.

Office Compatible button: Provides demonstrations on applications which are compatible with MS Office.

Answer Wizard button: Provides help on various topics which you might need while working with Office.

Starting the Excel Program

Excel is started in Windows 95 either by clicking the **Start** button then selecting **Program** and clicking on the 'Microsoft Excel' icon on the cascade menu, by clicking the Excel icon on the Old Office Shortcut Bar, or by clicking the 'Open a Document' icon on the Office Shortcut Bar and double-clicking on an Excel worksheet file. In the latter case the worksheet will be loaded into Excel at the same time.

The first time you use Excel you get the 'What's New' Help screen displayed. After that, to get back to this Help screen, use **Help, Answer Wizard** and type *what's new* in the Type Your Request box, then select What's New in Microsoft Excel 95. We suggest you spend a little time examining at least the first four options of this Help screen, shown below.

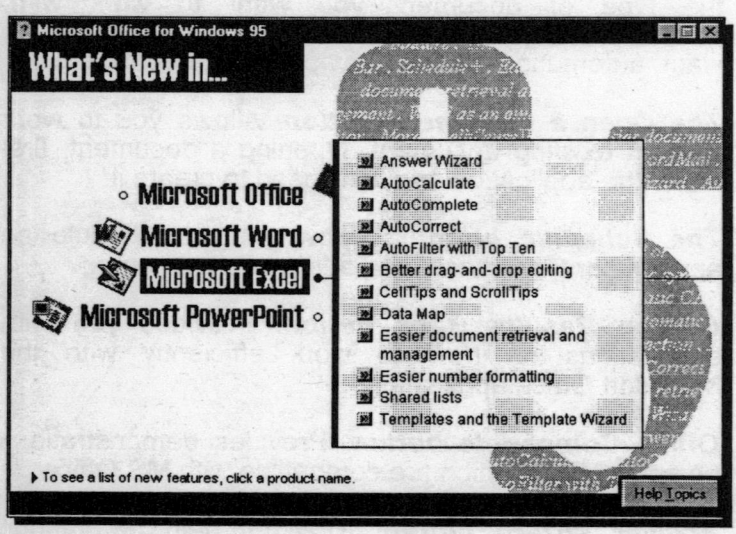

When Excel is loaded, a 'blank' spreadsheet screen displays with a similar Title bar, Menu bar, Toolbar and Formatting bar to those of Microsoft Word. Obviously there are some differences, but that is to be expected as the two programs serve different purposes.

The Excel Screen:

The opening screen of Excel is shown below. It is perhaps worth looking at the various parts that make up this screen, or window. Excel follows the usual Microsoft Windows 95 conventions with which you should be very familiar by now.

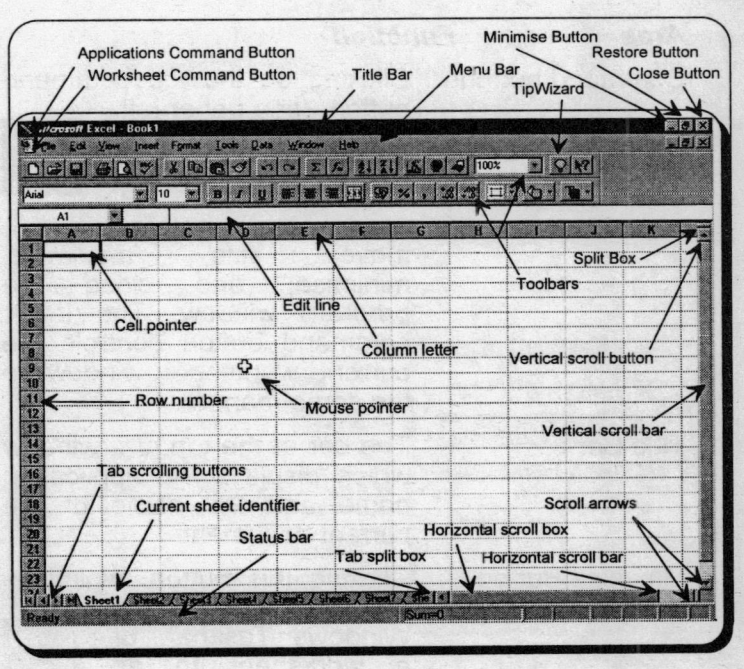

The window as shown takes up the full screen area available. If you click on the application restore button, the top one of the two restore buttons at the top right of the screen, you can make Excel show in a smaller window. This can be useful when you are running several applications at the same time and you want to transfer between them with the mouse.

Note that the Excel window, which in this case displays an empty and untitled book (Book1), has some areas which have identical functions to those of other Microsoft Office applications, and other areas which have different functions. Below, we describe first the areas that are common to other MS Office applications and then those that are exclusive to Excel.

Area	*Function*
Command buttons	Clicking on the top command button, (see upper-left corner of the window), displays a pull-down menu which can be used to restore, move, size, maximise, minimise, and close the program window. The lower command button controls the current worksheet window in the same manner.
Title Bar	The bar at the top of a window which displays the application name and the name of the current document.
Minimise Button	Clicking this button minimises the application to the Windows Taskbar, or a worksheet to an icon.

8

Restore Button	When clicked on, this button restores the active window to the position and size that was occupied before it was maximised. The restore button is then replaced by a Maximise button, as shown here, which is used to set the window to full screen size.
Close button	The extreme top right button that you click to close a window.
Menu Bar	The bar below the Title bar which allows you to choose from several menu options. Clicking on a menu item displays the pull-down menu associated with that item.
Toolbar	The bar below the Menu bar which contains buttons that give you mouse-click access to the functions most often used in the program. These are grouped according to function.
Formatting Bar	The buttons on the Formatting Bar allow you to change the attributes of a font, such as italic and underline, and also to format text in various ways. The Formatting Bar contains two boxes; a font box and a size box which show which font and size of characters are currently being used. These boxes give access to other installed fonts and character sizes.

9

Ruler	The area where you can see and set tabulation points and indents.
Split Box	The area above the top vertical scroll button which when dragged allows you to split the screen.
Scroll Bars	The areas on the screen (extreme right and bottom of each window) that contain scroll boxes in vertical and horizontal bars. Clicking on these bars allows you to control the part of a document which is visible on the screen.
Scroll Arrows	The arrowheads at each end of each scroll bar at which you can click to scroll the screen up and down one line, or left and right 10% of the screen, at a time.
Status Bar	The bottom line of the document window that displays status information, and in which a short help description appears when you point and click on a button.
TipWizard	The bulb icon which lights up if there is a quicker or more efficient way of performing the action you have just performed. Clicking on the icon displays the tip, while clicking on the icon once more removes it.
Edit line	Contains the selection indicator (cell co-ordinates), and the name box that identifies the

10

	selected cell, chart item, or drawing object. The edit line box can display a number, a label, or the formula behind a result.
Cell pointer	Marks the current cell.
Column letter	The letter that identifies each column.
Row number	The number that identifies each row.
Tab scrolling	Clicking on these buttons, scrolls sheet tabs right or left, when there are more tabs than can be displayed at once.
Current sheet	Shows the current sheet amongst a number of sheets in a file. These are named Sheet1, Sheet2, Sheet3, and so on, by default, but can be changed to, say, North, South, East, and West. Clicking on a sheet tab, moves you to that sheet.
Tab split box	The split box which you drag left to see more of the scroll bar, or right to see more tabs.

There is an extra split box on Excel's worksheet screen which has not been identified on the screen dump. This is located at the extreme bottom-right corner of the screen, to the left of the 'right horizontal scroll arrow' button. The one identified on the screen dump is located at the extreme right of the screen above the 'top vertical scroll arrow' button. Both of these have to do with splitting the screen; the identified one horizontally, the other vertically. The use of both these split boxes will be discussed later.

The Menu Bar Options:

Each menu bar option has associated with it a pull-down sub-menu. To activate the menu, either press the <Alt> key, which causes the first option of the menu (in this case the current Book Control Menu box) to be highlighted, then use the right and left arrow keys to highlight any of the options in the menu, or use the mouse to point to an option. Pressing either the <Enter> key, or the left mouse button, reveals the pull-down sub-menu of the highlighted menu option.

Menu options can also be activated directly by pressing the <Alt> key followed by the underlined letter of the required option. Thus, pressing <Alt+F>, causes the pull-down sub-menu of the **File** menu to be displayed, as shown here. You can use the up and down arrow keys to move the highlighted bar up and down a sub-menu, or the right and left arrow keys to move along the options in the menu bar.

As you move up and down a sub-menu, a brief description of the highlighted option appears in the Status bar. Pressing the <Enter> key selects the option or executes the option command. Pressing the <Esc> key once, closes the pull-down sub-menu, while pressing it a second time, closes the menu system.

Some sub-menu options can be accessed from the keyboard with 'quick key' combinations which are shown on the drop-down menus. If a sub-menu option is not available, at any time, it will display in a grey colour. Some menu options only appear in Excel when that tool or command is being used.

The Mouse Pointers:

In Microsoft Excel, as with all other graphical based programs, the use of a mouse makes many operations both easier and more fun to carry out.

Excel makes use of the mouse pointers available in Windows 95, some of the most common of which are illustrated below. When Excel is initially started up the first you will see is the hourglass which, once the application screen appears on your display, turns into either an upward pointing hollow arrow or a hollow cross, depending on the area you point to. Other shapes depend on the type of work you are doing at the time.

The hourglass which displays when you are waiting while performing a function.

The arrow which appears when the pointer is placed over menus, toolbars, scrolling bars, and buttons.

The hollow cross which appears when the pointer is placed within the worksheet area.

The I-beam which appears when editing a cell or in text areas of the screen.

The large 4-headed arrow which appears after choosing the **Control, Move/Size** command(s) for moving or sizing windows.

The double arrows which appear when over the border of a window, used to drag the side and alter the size of the window.

The Help hand which appears in the Help windows, and is used to access 'hypertext' type links.

Excel, like other Windows applications, has additional mouse pointers which facilitate the execution of selected commands. The shape of some pointers is mostly self-evident, while others, shown below, have the following functions:

↓   The vertical pointer which appears when pointing over a column in a worksheet and used to select the column.

→   The horizontal pointer which appears when pointing at a row in a worksheet and used to select the row.

◄‖►   The vertical split arrow which appears when pointing at the vertical split box or over the area separating two columns in a worksheet and used to either split the screen or size a column.

≑   The horizontal split arrow which appears when pointing at the horizontal split box or over the area separating two rows in a worksheet and used to either split the screen or size the row.

+   The frame cross which you drag to create a frame.

∥   The draw pointer which appears when you are drawing freehand.

Using Help in Excel

The Microsoft Excel Help Program provides on-line help. You can use the **Help, Microsoft Excel Help Topics** command, then click the Contents tab, to obtain the following:

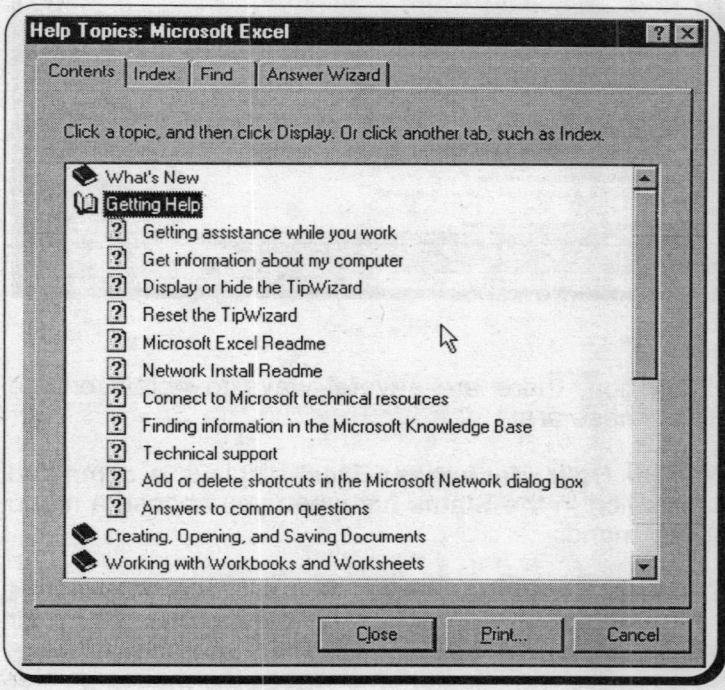

Help topics can be printed on paper by selecting the topic, then clicking the **Print** button.

Another way of obtaining help on a specific topic is to select the Answer Wizard, either by clicking its tab on the above window, or selecting it from the **Help** menu. You can then type your request in the top box and click the **Search** button, which lists the available information in the second box, as shown overleaf.

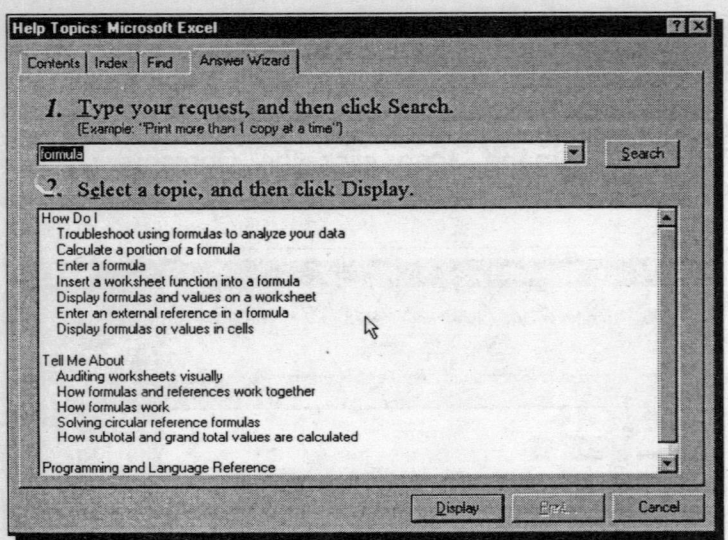

In addition, there are several ways to obtain on-line Help. These are:

On-line Help Messages: Excel displays a command description in the Status bar when you choose a menu or command.

Context Sensitive Help: Some Excel operations display a '?' button on the right end of their dialogue box or window, as shown here. Clicking this button changes the mouse pointer from its usual inclined arrow shape to the 'What's this?' shape. Pointing to an object in the dialogue box or window and clicking the left mouse button, opens a Help topic.

2. THE EXCEL WORKSHEET

When you first enter Excel, the program sets up a series of huge electronic pages, or worksheets, in your computer's memory, many times larger than the small part shown on the screen. Individual cells are identified by column and row location (in that order), with present size extending to 256 columns and 16,384 rows. The columns are labelled from A to Z, followed by AA to AZ, BA to BZ, and so on, to IV, while the rows are numbered from 1 to 16,384.

Workbook Navigation

A worksheet can be thought of as a two-dimensional table made up of rows and columns. The point where a row and column intersect is called a cell, while the reference points of a cell are known as the cell address. The active cell (A1 when you first enter the program) is boxed.

Navigation around the worksheet is achieved by using one of the following keys or key combinations:

- Pressing one of the four arrow keys (→↓←↑) moves the active cell one position right, down, left or up, respectively.

- Pressing the <PgDn> or <PgUp> keys moves the active cell down or up one visible page.

- Pressing the <Ctrl+→> or <Ctrl+↓> key combinations moves the active cell to the extreme right of the worksheet (column IV) or extreme bottom of the worksheet (row 16,384).

- Pressing the <Home> key, moves the active cell to the beginning of a row.

- Pressing the <Ctrl+Home> key combination moves the active cell to the home position, A1.

- Pressing the <Ctrl+End> key combination moves the active cell to the lower right corner of the worksheet's currently used area.

- Pressing the **F5** function key will display the Go To dialogue box shown below.

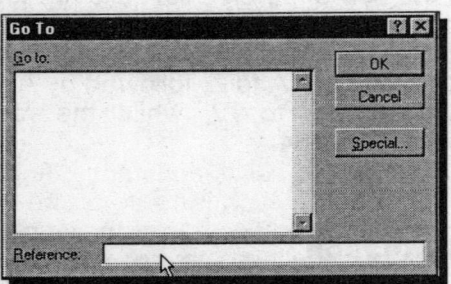

In the **Go to** box a list of named ranges in the active worksheet (to be discussed shortly) is displayed, or one of the last four references from which you chose the **Go To** command.

In the **Reference** box you type the cell reference or a named range you want to move to.

To move the active cell with a mouse, do the following:

- Point to the cell you want to move to and click the left mouse button. If the cell is not visible, move the window by clicking on the scroll bar arrowhead that points in the direction you want to move.

- To move a page at a time, click in the scroll bar itself.

- For larger moves, drag the box in the scroll bar, but the distances moved will depend on the size of the worksheet.

When you have finished navigating around the worksheet, press the <Ctrl+Home> key combination which will move the active cell to the A1 position (provided you have not fixed titles in any rows or columns or have no hidden rows or columns - more about these later).

Note that the area within which you can move the active cell is referred to as the working area of the worksheet, while the letters and numbers in the border at the top and left of the working area give the 'co-ordinates' of the cells in a worksheet.

The location of the active cell is constantly monitored by the 'selection indicator' which is to be found on the extreme left below the lower Toolbar of the application window. As the active cell is moved, this indicator displays its address, as shown below.

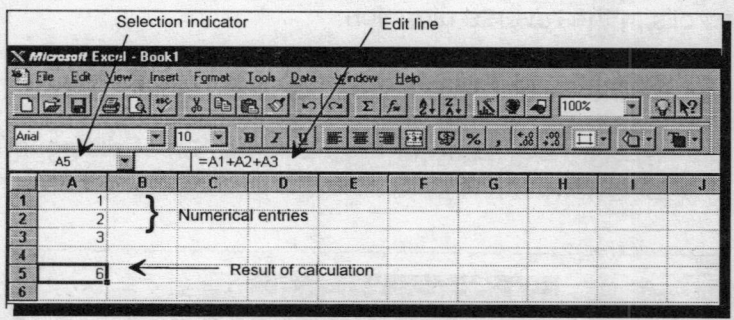

The contents of a cell are displayed above the column letters within what is known as the 'Edit line'. If you type text in the active cell, what you type appears in both the 'Edit line' and the cell itself.

Typing a formula which is preceded by the equals sign (=) to, say, add the contents of three cells, causes the actual formula to appear in the 'Edit line', while the result of the actual calculation appears in the active cell when the <Enter> key is pressed.

Moving Between Sheets:

You can scroll between sheets by clicking one of the arrows situated to the left of Sheet 1, as shown below. We have labelled these as 'Tab scrolling buttons'. The inner arrows scroll sheets one at a time in the direction of the arrow, while the outer arrows scroll to the end, or beginning, of the group of available sheets. A sheet is then made current by clicking its tab.

With the keyboard, you can scroll one sheet at a time, and make it active at the same time, by using the <Ctrl+PgDn> key combination. Using <Ctrl+PgUp> scrolls in the reverse direction.

To display more sheet tabs at a time, drag the split box to the right. The reverse action displays fewer sheet tabs. To rename sheets, double-click at their tab, then type a new name in the Rename Sheet dialogue box, as shown below.

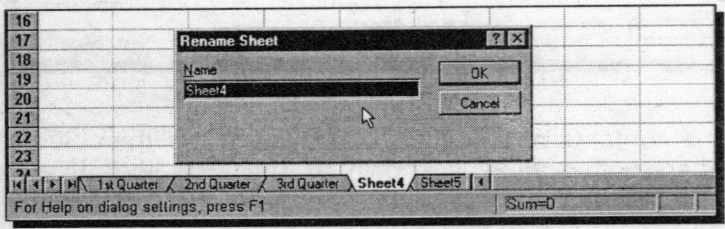

To insert a sheet in front of a certain sheet, make that sheet current, then use the **Insert, Worksheet** command sequence. To delete a sheet, make it current and use the **Edit, Delete Sheet** command sequence.

Rearranging Sheet Order:

If you need to rearrange the order in which sheets are being held in a workbook, you can do so by dragging a particular sheet to its new position, as shown below.

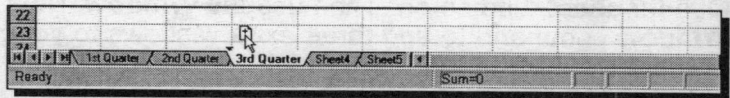

While you are dragging the tab of the sheet you want to move, the mouse pointer changes to an arrow pointing to a sheet. The small solid arrowhead to the left of the mouse pointer indicates the place where the sheet you are moving will be placed.

Grouping Worksheets:

You can select several sheets to group them together so that data entry, editing, or formatting can be made easier and more consistent.

To select adjacent sheets, click the first sheet tab, hold down the <Shift> key and then click the last sheet tab in the group. To select non-adjacent sheets, click the first sheet tab, hold down the <Ctrl> key and then click the other sheet tabs you want to group together.

Selecting sheets in the above manner, causes the word '[Group]' to appear in the Title bar of the active window, and the tabs of the selected sheets to be shown in white. To cancel the selection, click at the tab of any sheet which is not part of the selected group.

Shortcut Menus:

While a range of cells in a sheet is selected, or a group of sheets is active, you can access a shortcut menu of relevant commands by pressing the right mouse button. This produces a shortcut menu of the most common commands relevant to what you are doing at the time.

Viewing Multiple Workbook Sheets

To see more clearly what you are doing when starting with multiple workbook sheets, type the text '1st' in location A1 of 1st Quarter sheet, '2nd' in the 2nd Quarter sheet, and so on. Then use the **Window, New Window** command to add three extra windows to your worksheet, and the **Window, Arrange, Tiled** command to display the four sheets as shown below.

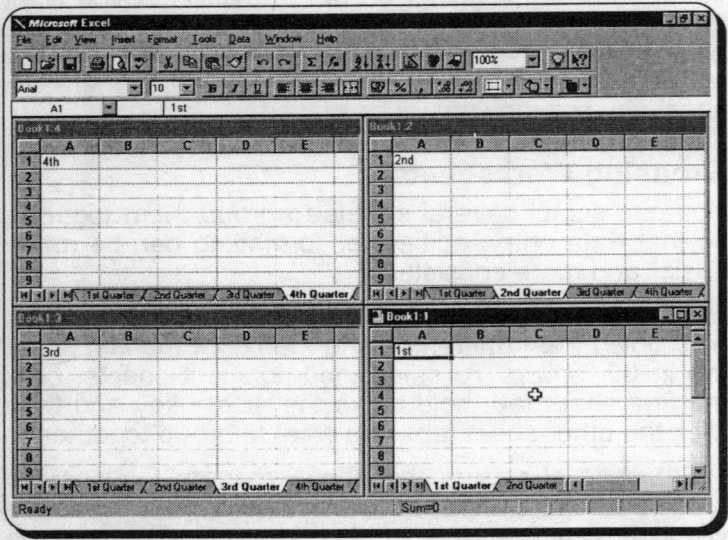

To move from one window to another, simply point with the mouse to the cell of the window you want to go to and click the left mouse button. To display a different sheet in each window, go to a window and click the sheet's tab.

To return to single-window view mode from a tiled or cascade mode, click the maximise button of the active window.

Using Styles and Templates

Excel 95 allows you to define and save combinations of formats, such as font size, patterns, and alignments, as a style, then apply this style to another workbook. New workbooks are opened with the default built-in **Normal** style, as shown below by using the **Format, Style** command.

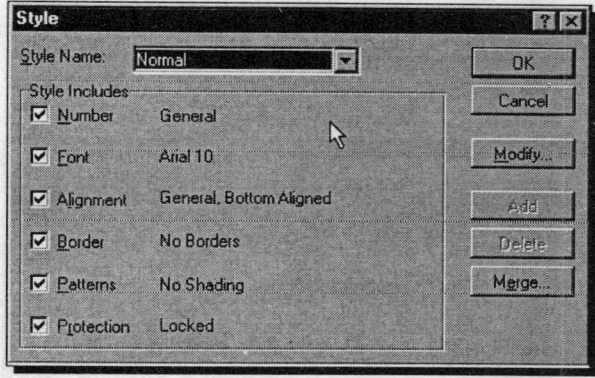

To change a style, press the **Modify** button to display the dialogue box below.

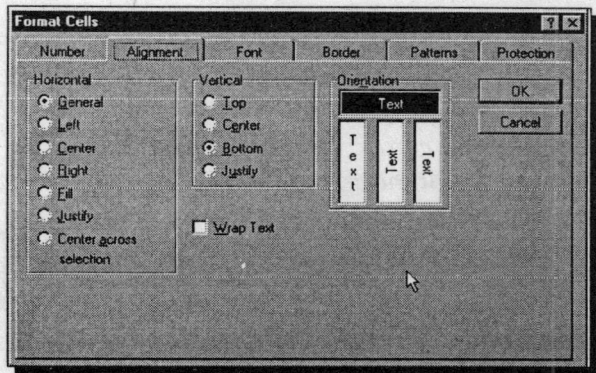

In the Format Cells dialogue box you can change the Numbers format, Alignment of text, Font size, borders and Patterns of cells, and Protection, by simply clicking the appropriate tab on the dialogue box and making the required changes.

A modified style can be given a name by returning to the Style dialogue box and typing a new name in place of the current named style (we typed **MyStyle**). To apply a new style to a range of cells, highlight the range and use the **Format, Style** command, then select the required style from the drop-down list of styles, as shown below, and press **OK**.

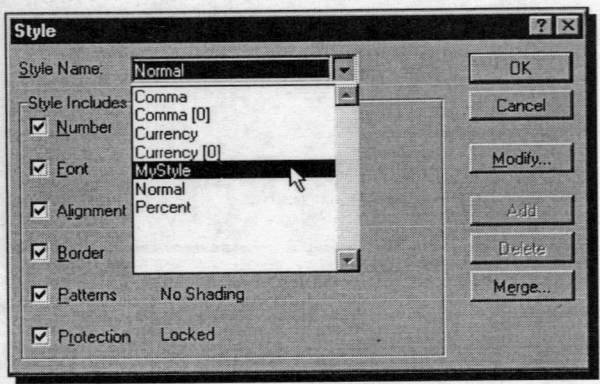

Templates are special workbooks that you can use as a pattern to create other workbooks. They can contain text, graphics, formatting instructions, macros, and styles.

To create a workbook template, do the following:

- Create a workbook that contains the sheets, default text (such as column headings), formulae, macros, styles, and other formatting you want in new workbooks.

- On the **File** menu, click **Save As**.

- In the File Name dialogue box, type the template name.

- In the **Save in** box, click the Templates folder in the folder in which you installed Excel or Microsoft Office.

- In the **Save as type** box, click Template.

If you followed all the steps given above, your screen should display the following.

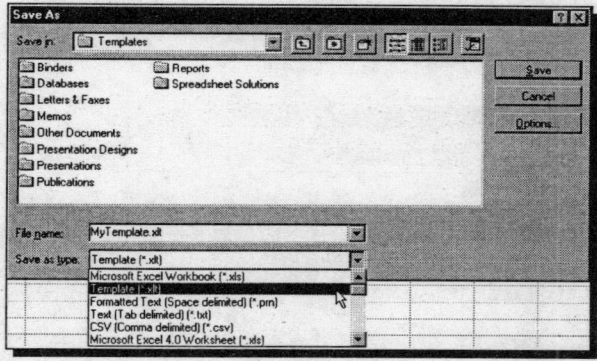

Once you get accustomed to using styles and templates, you will find it saves you an enormous amount of time with document formatting, which will be discussed in some detail later.

3. FILLING IN A WORKSHEET

Entering Information

We will now investigate how information can be entered into a worksheet. But first, make sure you are in Sheet1, then return to the Home (A1) position, by pressing the <Ctrl+Home> key combination, then type the words:

```
PROJECT ANALYSIS
```

As you type, the characters appear in both the 'Edit line' and the active cell. If you make a mistake, press the <BkSp> key to erase the previous letter or the <Esc> key to start again. When you have finished, press <Enter>.

Note that what you have just typed in has been entered in cell A1, even though the whole of the word ANALYSIS appears to be in cell B1. If you use the right arrow key to move the active cell to B1 you will see that the cell is indeed empty.

Typing any letter at the beginning of an entry into a cell results in a 'text' entry being formed automatically, otherwise known as a 'label'. If the length of the text is longer than the width of a cell, it will continue into the next cell to the right of the current active cell, provided that cell is empty, otherwise the displayed information will be truncated.

To edit information already in a cell, either

- double-click the cell in question, or
- make that cell the active cell and press the **F2** function key.

The cursor keys, the <Home> and <End> keys, as well as the <Ins> and <Del> keys can be used to move the cursor and/or edit information as required.

You can also 'undo' the most recent operation, carried out since the program was last in the **Ready** mode, by using the **Edit, Undo Entry** command.

Next, use the arrow keys to move the active cell to B3 and type

```
Jan
```

Pressing the right arrow key (→) will automatically enter the typed information into the cell and also move the active cell one cell to the right, in this case to C3. Now type

```
Feb
```

and press <Enter>.

The looks of a worksheet can be enhanced somewhat by using different types of borders around specific cells. To do this, first select the range of cells (as discussed below), then click at the down arrow of the Borders icon on the Formatting Toolbar, shown here, which displays a choice of twelve different types of borders, as shown below.

Selecting a Range of Cells:

To select a range of cells, say, A3:C3, point to cell A3, then

• press the left mouse button, and while holding it pressed, drag the mouse to the right.

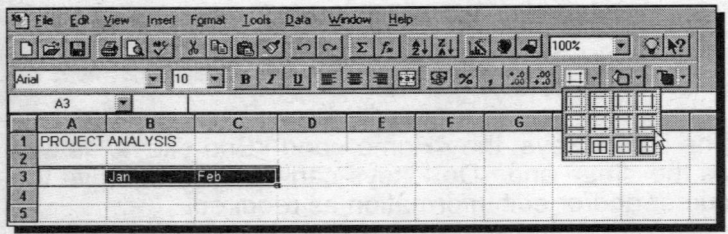

In our example, we have selected the cell range A3:C3, then we chose the 8th border from the display table.

To select a range from the keyboard, first make active the first cell in the range, then

- hold down the <Shift> key and use the right arrow key (→) to highlight the required range.

To select a 3D range, across several sheets, select the range in the first sheet, then

- release the mouse button, hold down the <Shift> key, and click the Tab of the last sheet in the range.

To continue with our example, move to cell A4 and type the label Income, then enter the numbers 14000 and 15000 in cells B4 and C4, respectively. What you should have on your screen now, is shown below.

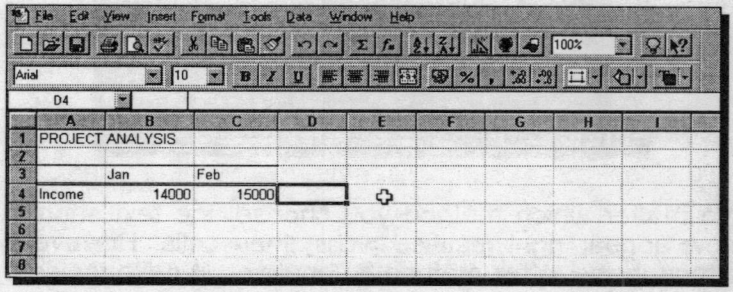

Note how the labels 'Jan' and 'Feb' do not appear above the numbers 14000 and 15000. This is because by default, labels are left justified, while numbers are right justified.

Changing Text Alignment and Fonts:

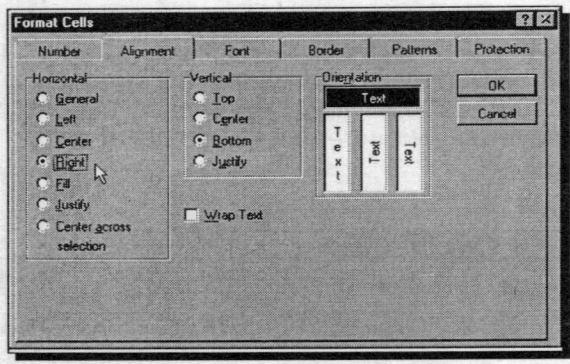

One way of improving the looks of this worksheet is to also right justify the text 'Jan' and 'Feb' within their respective cells. To do this, move the active cell to B3 and select the range B3 to C3 by dragging the mouse, then either click the 'Align Right' icon, shown here, or choose the

Format, **Cells**

command, then select the **Alignment** tab from the displayed Format Cells dialogue box, shown below, choose the **Right** button from the list under **Horizontal**, and press **OK**.

No matter which method you choose, the text should now appear right justified within their cells. However, although the latter method is lengthier, it nevertheless provides you with greater flexibility in displaying text, both in terms of position and orientation.

We could further improve the looks of our worksheet by choosing a different font for the heading 'Project Analysis'. To achieve this, select cell A1, then click on the 'Font Size' button on the second Toolbar, to reveal the band of available point sizes for the selected font, as shown overleaf. From this band, choose 14, then click in succession the 'Bold' and 'Italic' icons.

Finally, since the numbers in cells B4 to C4 represent money, it would be better if these were prefixed with the £ sign. To do this, select the cell range B4:C4, then either click the 'Currency Style' button on the second Toolbar, shown here, or choose the

Format, Style

command and select **Currency** from the list under **Style Name** in the displayed Style dialogue box.

The numbers within the chosen range will now be displayed in currency form, provided the width of the cells is sufficient to accommodate them. In our example, the entered numbers are far too long to fit in currency form in the default cell width and appear as shown under the 'Feb' entry.

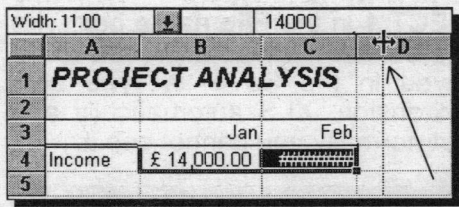

To see the actual numbers we must increase the width of the columns B4:C4 to 11 characters wide (as shown at the top left of the adjacent display). To do this, place the mouse pointer in between the column letters on the dividing line, and drag the pointer to the right, as pointed to above, until the width of the column is displayed as 11.00. The resultant worksheet should look as follows:

	A	B	C	D	E	F	G	H	I	
1	PROJECT ANALYSIS									
2										
3		Jan	Feb							
4	Income	£ 14,000.00	£15,000.00							
5										

31

Saving a Workbook

Now, let us assume that we would like to stop at this point, but would also like to save the work entered so far before leaving the program. First, return to the Home position by pressing <Ctrl+Home>. This is good practice because when a workbook is opened later, the position of the cell pointer at the time of saving the file appears at the top left corner of the opened worksheet which might cause confusion if below and to the right of it there are no entries - you might think that you opened an empty worksheet.

Next, choose the

File, Save

command to reveal the Save As dialogue box, select to save your work in the **a:** drive, and type the new name of the file, say, **PROJECT 1** in the **File name** box. The file will be saved in the default file type *Microsoft Excel Workbook*, as displayed in the **Save as type** box. Excel adds the file extension **.XLS** automatically and uses it to identify it, but normally you cannot see it.

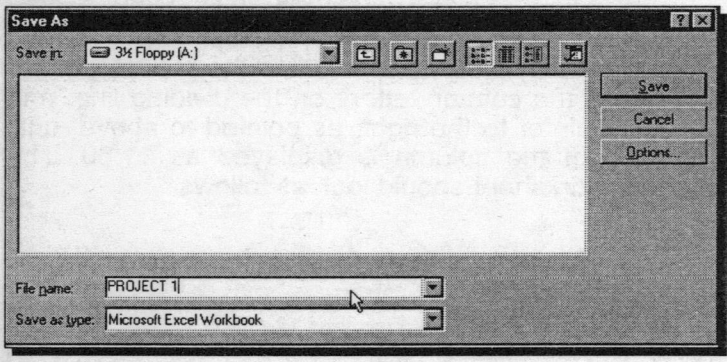

If you want to create backup files or provide password protection to your file, click the **Options** button. Clicking the **Save** button, causes the file to be saved under the chosen name.

Opening a Workbook

An already saved workbook, or file, can be opened by
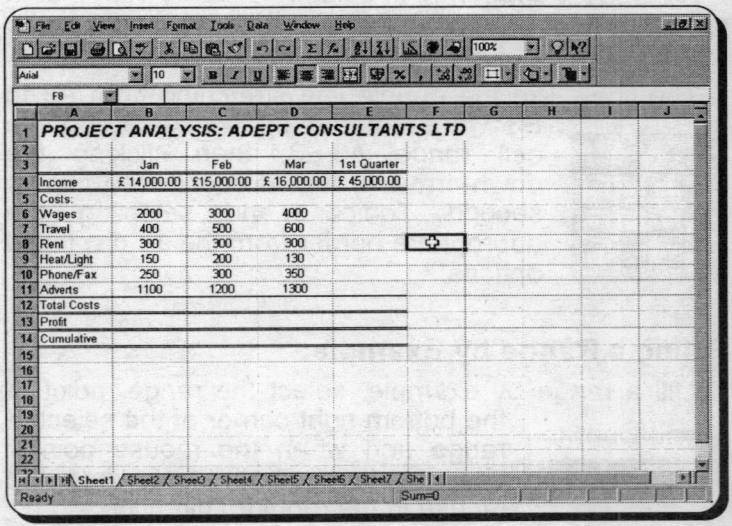 either clicking at the 'Open' icon, shown here,
or selecting the

File, Open

command which displays the Open dialogue box. Do
not forget to change the drive to **a:**, if that is where you
saved your work (by selecting Floppy (A:) in the **Look
in** box drop-down list). Excel asks for a filename to
open, with the default *Microsoft Excel Files* being
displayed in the **Files of type** box. If the file was
saved, select it by clicking its name in the list box, then
click the **Open** button. If you haven't saved it, don't
worry as you could just as easily start afresh.

Next use the **F2** function key to 'Edit' existing entries
or simply retype the contents of cells (see below for
formatting) so that your worksheet looks as follows:

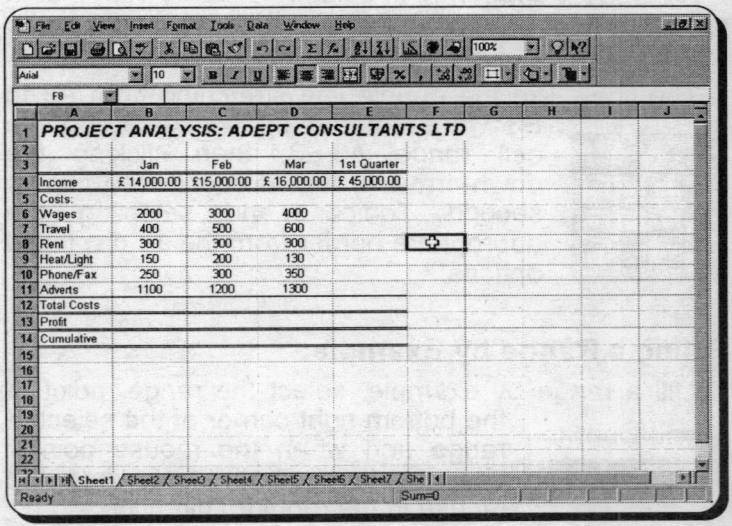

Formatting Entries

The information in cell A1 (PROJECT ANALYSIS: ADEPT CONSULTANTS LTD) was entered left justified and formatted by clicking on the 'Font Size' button on the Formatting Toolbar, and selecting 14 point font size from the band of available font sizes, then clicking in succession the 'Bold' and 'Italic' icons.

The text in the cell block B3:E3 was formatted by first selecting the range and then clicking the 'Centre' alignment icon on the second Toolbar, so the text within the range was displayed centre justified.

The numbers within the cell block B4:E4 were formatted by first selecting the range, then clicking the 'Currency Style' icon on the second Toolbar, shown here, so the numbers appeared with two digits after the decimal point and prefixed with the £ sign.

All the text appearing in column A (apart from that in cell A1) was just typed in (left justified), as shown in the screen dump on the previous page.

The lines, like the double line stretching from A3 to E3 were entered by first selecting the cell range A3:E3, then clicking the down-arrow of the 'Borders' icon on the second Toolbar, and selecting the appropriate border from the 12 displayed options.

Filling a Range by Example:

To fill a range by example, select the range, point at the bottom right corner of the selected range and when the mouse pointer changes to a small cross, drag the mouse in the required direction.

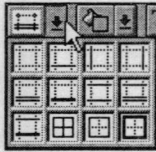

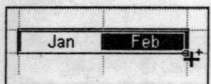

In the previous case, the next cell to the right will automatically fill with the text 'Mar' (Excel anticipates that you want to fill cells by example with the abbreviations for months, and does it for you). Not only that, but it also copies the format of the selected range forward. It is, therefore, evident that selecting ranges and using icons makes various tasks a lot easier.

Microsoft Excel allows you to format both text (labels) and numbers in any way you choose. For example, you can have numbers centre justified in their cells.

Entering Text, Numbers and Formulae:

When text, a number, a formula, or an Excel function is entered into a cell, or reference is made to the contents of a cell by the cell address, then the content of the status bar changes from **Ready** to **Enter**. This status can be changed back to **Ready** by either completing an entry and pressing <Enter> or one of the arrow keys, or by pressing <Esc>.

We can find the 1st quarter total income from consultancy, by activating cell E4, typing

=B4+C4+D4

and pressing <Enter>. The total first quarter income is added, using the above formula, and the result is placed in cell E4.

Now complete the insertion into the spreadsheet of the various amounts under 'costs' and then choose the

File, Save As

command to save the resultant worksheet under the filename **PROJECT 2**, before going on any further. Remember that saving your work on disc often enough is a good thing to get used to, as even the shortest power cut can cause the loss of hours of hard work!

Using Functions

In our example, writing a formula that adds the contents of three columns is not too difficult or lengthy a task. But imagine having to add 20 columns! For this reason Excel has an in-built summation function which can be used to add any number of columns (or rows).

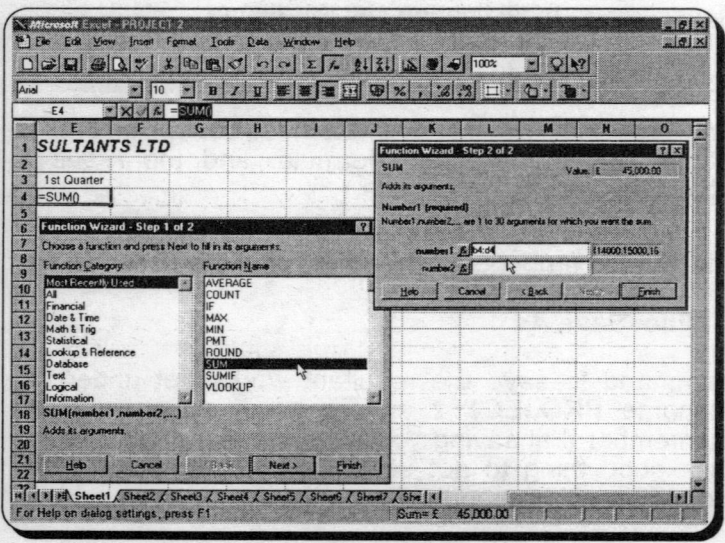

To illustrate how this and other functions can be used, activate cell E4 and press the Function Wizard button shown here. If the function you require appears on the displayed dialogue box under **Function Name**, choose it, otherwise select the appropriate class from the list under **Function Category**.

Choosing the **SUM** function, inserts the entry SUM(number1,number2,...) in the Edit line. Clicking the **Next** button, causes the appearance of a second dialogue box, as shown in the composite screen dump below, which allows you to insert the range over which the function is to be effective.

In this case, we enter B4:D4 and click **OK**, as the range we want to summate is continuous. If the range is not continuous, separate the various continuous portions of it with a comma (,).

Pressing <Enter> or clicking the **Finish** button causes the result of the calculation to appear in the active cell.

Using the AutoSum Icon:

With addition, there is a better and quicker way of letting Excel work out the desired result. To illustrate this, select the cell range B6:E12, which contains the 'Costs' we would like to add up. To add these in both the horizontal and vertical direction, we include in the selected range an empty column to the right of the numbers and an empty row below the numbers, as shown below.

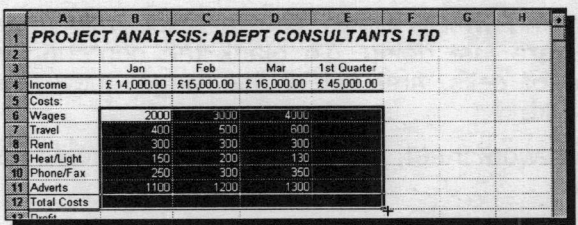

Pressing the 'AutoSum' icon, shown here, inserts the result of the summations in the empty column and row, as shown below. The selected range remains selected so that any other formatting can be applied by simply pressing the appropriate icon button.

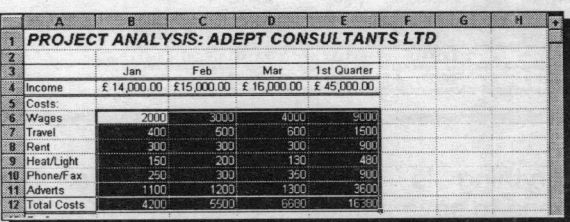

Now complete the insertion of formulae in the rest of the worksheet, noting that 'Profit', in B13, is the difference between 'Income' and 'Total Cost', calculated by the formula **=B4–B12**. To complete the entry, this formula should be copied using the 'fill by example' method into the three cells to its right.

The 'Cumulative' entry in cell B14 should be a simple reference to cell B13, that is **=B13**, while in cell C14 it should be **=B14+C13**. Similarly, the latter formula is copied into cell D14 using the 'fill by example' method.

Finally, format the entire range B6:E12 as currency, by selecting the range and clicking the 'Currency Style' button.

If you make any mistakes and copy formats or information into cells you did not mean to, use the

Edit, Undo

command which allows you to selectively undo what you were just doing. To blank the contents within a range of cells, first select the range, then press the <Del> key.

The worksheet, up to this point, should look as follows:

	A	B	C	D	E	F	G	H
1	*PROJECT ANALYSIS: ADEPT CONSULTANTS LTD*							
2								
3		Jan	Feb	Mar	1st Quarter			
4	Income	£ 14,000.00	£15,000.00	£ 16,000.00	£ 45,000.00			
5	Costs:							
6	Wages	£ 2,000.00	£ 3,000.00	£ 4,000.00	£ 9,000.00			
7	Travel	£ 400.00	£ 500.00	£ 600.00	£ 1,500.00			
8	Rent	£ 300.00	£ 300.00	£ 300.00	£ 900.00			
9	Heat/Light	£ 150.00	£ 200.00	£ 130.00	£ 480.00		⇔	
10	Phone/Fax	£ 250.00	£ 300.00	£ 350.00	£ 900.00			
11	Adverts	£ 1,100.00	£ 1,200.00	£ 1,300.00	£ 3,600.00			
12	Total Costs	£ 4,200.00	£ 5,500.00	£ 6,680.00	£ 16,380.00			
13	Profit	£ 9,800.00	£ 9,500.00	£ 9,320.00	£ 28,620.00			
14	Cumulative	£ 9,800.00	£19,300.00	£ 28,620.00				
15								

If everything is correct, use the **File, Save As** command to save it under the filename **PROJECT 3**.

Printing a Worksheet

To print a worksheet, make sure that the printer you propose to use was defined when you first installed Windows 95.

If you have named more than one printer in your original installation of Windows, and want to select a printer other than your original first choice, then select the **File, Print** command, click the down-arrow against the **Name** box on the displayed Print dialogue box and select the required printer, as shown below.

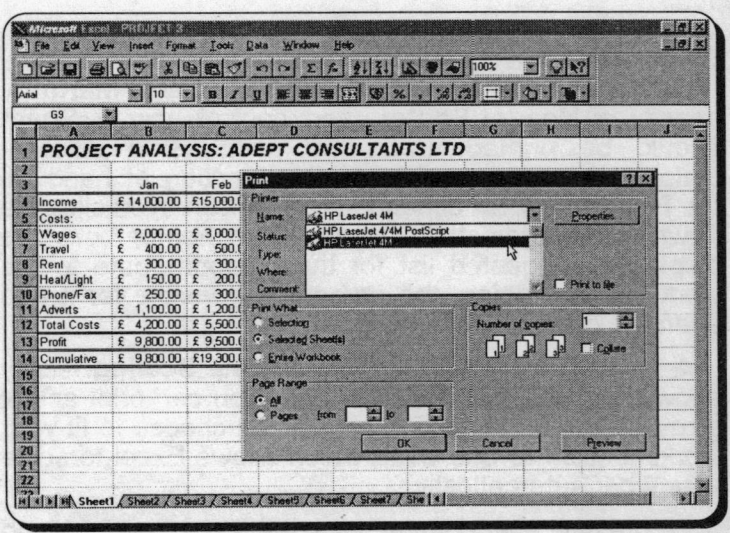

If you want to change the paper size, print orientation or printer resolution, click the **Properties** button on the Print dialogue box. These and other changes to the appearance of the printout can also be made by choosing the **File, Page Setup** command which causes the Page Setup dialogue box to be displayed, as shown overleaf.

39

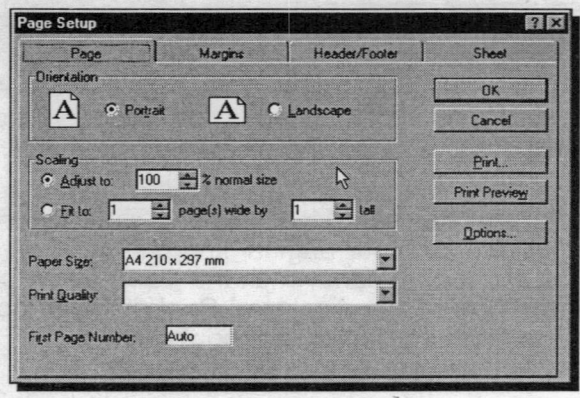

By selecting the appropriate Tab on this dialogue box, you can change your **Page** settings, page **Margins**, specify a **Header/Footer**, and control how a **Sheet** should be printed. Each Tab displays a different dialogue box, appropriate to the function at hand. In the **Header/Footer** dialogue box you can even click the down-arrow against the Header and Footer boxes to display a suggested list for these, appropriate to the work you are doing, the person responsible for it and even the date it is being carried out! Try it.

A very useful feature of Excel is the **Scaling** facility shown in the above dialogue box. You can print actual size or a percentage of it, or you can choose to fit your worksheet on to one page which allows Excel to scale your work automatically.

To preview a worksheet, click the 'Print Preview' icon on the Toolbar, shown here, or click the **Print Preview** button on the Page Setup dialogue box, or the **Preview** button on the Print dialogue box. You can even use the **File, Print Preview** command!

The idea of all these preview choices is to make it easy for you to see your work on screen before committing it to paper, thus saving a few trees.

4. ADVANCED SPREADSHEETS

Enhancing a Worksheet

You can make your work look more professional by adopting various enhancements, such as single and double line cell borders, shading certain cells, and adding meaningful headers and footers.

However, with Excel you can easily select a pre-defined style to display your work on both the screen and on paper. To do this, place the active cell within the table (or range) you want to format, say C5, then select the **Format, AutoFormat** which will cause the following dialogue box to appear on the screen, displaying a sample of the chosen table format. In this way you can choose what best suits your needs. We selected 'Classic 2' and pressed **OK**.

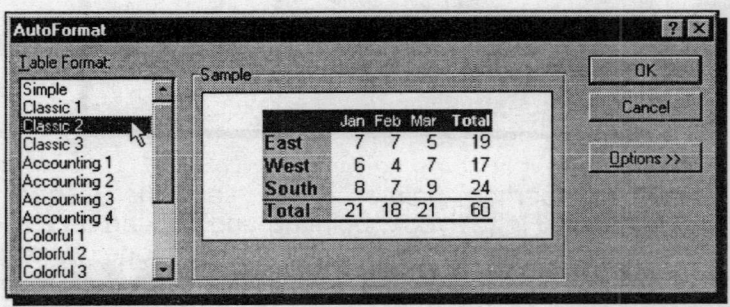

Next, reduce the title of the worksheet to PROJECT ANALYSIS, then centre it within the range A1:E1, by first selecting the range, then clicking the 'Centre Across Columns' icon, shown here, which causes the title to centre within the specified range.

Finally, save the worksheet as **PROJECT 4**, before going on.

Header and Footer Icons and Codes:

With the help of header and footer icons and their codes, shown below, you can position text or automatically insert information at the top or bottom of a report printout.

To add a header to our printed example, use the **File, Page Setup** command and click on the **Header/Footer** Tab, press the **Custom Header** button and type the information displayed below in the Left Section and Right Section of the Header box:

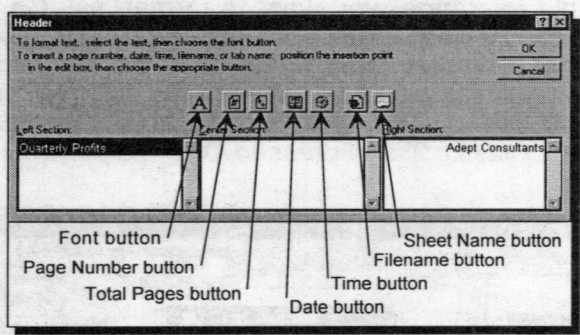

While the insertion pointer is in, say, the Centre Section of the Header box, pointing and clicking on the 'Sheet Name' button, inserts the &[Tab] code which has the effect of inserting the sheet name of the current active sheet at the time of printing. The first icon button displays the Font dialogue box, while the others display the codes listed below.

Code	*Action*
&[Page]	Inserts a page number.
&[Pages]	Inserts the total number of pages.
&[Date]	Inserts the current date.
&[Time]	Inserts the current time.
&[File]	Inserts the filename of the current workbook.

Setting a Print Area:

To choose a smaller print area than the current worksheet, select the required area by highlighting the starting cell of the area and dragging the mouse, or using the **<Shift+Arrows>**, to highlight the block, and use the **File, Print** command which displays the following dialogue box:

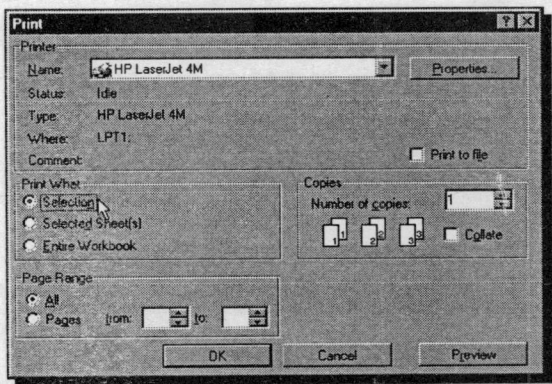

Choose the **Selection** button in the **Print What** box, and either click the **Preview** or the **OK** button to preview your report on screen or print it on paper. Once in preview mode, the following icons are available to you.

The first two allow you to change sheets, while the next one allows you to review your print output magnified or at full page size - when in full page size, the mouse pointer looks like a magnifying glass, as above. The next three icons can be used to print, change page settings, or to display and change the margins. To leave the preview option, press the **Close** button.

Another way to set the area to print is using the **File, Print Area, Set Print Area** menu command.

To print selected sheets or the entire workbook, click the appropriate button in the **Print What** box of the Print dialogue box.

The default selection in the **Print What** box is **Selecte_d Sheet(s)** which is also what will be printed out if you click the 'Print' icon, shown here.

If you have included headers and footers, these will be printed out irrespective of whether you choose to print a selected range or a selected worksheet.

Printing our worksheet produces the following page:

Quarterly Profits				Adept Consultants
	Jan	Feb	Mar	1st Quarter
Income	£14,000.00	£15,000.00	£16,000.00	£45,000.00
Costs:				
Wages	£ 2,000.00	£ 3,000.00	£ 4,000.00	£ 9,000.00
Travel	£ 400.00	£ 500.00	£ 600.00	£ 1,500.00
Rent	£ 300.00	£ 300.00	£ 300.00	£ 900.00
Heat/Light	£ 150.00	£ 200.00	£ 130.00	£ 480.00
Phone/Fax	£ 250.00	£ 300.00	£ 350.00	£ 900.00
Adverts	£ 1,100.00	£ 1,200.00	£ 1,300.00	£ 3,600.00
Total Costs	£ 4,200.00	£ 5,500.00	£ 6,680.00	£16,380.00
Profit	£ 9,800.00	£ 9,500.00	£ 9,320.00	£28,620.00
Cumulative	£ 9,800.00	£19,300.00	£28,620.00	

5/1/96

Page 1

3-Dimensional Worksheets

In Excel, a Workbook is a 3-dimensional file made up with a series of flat 2-dimensional sheets stacked 'on top of each other'. Each sheet is the same size, and in itself, behaves the same as the more ordinary worksheets. As mentioned previously, each separate sheet in a file has its own Tab identifier at the bottom of the screen. Ranges can be set to span several different sheets to build up 3-dimensional blocks of data. These blocks can then be manipulated, copied, or moved to other locations in the file. A cell can reference any other cell in the file, no matter what sheet it is on, and an extended range of functions can be used to process these 3-dimensional ranges.

Manipulating Ranges:

The best way to demonstrate a new idea is to work through an example. We will use the worksheet saved under **PROJECT 4** (see end of previous chapter). Next, start Excel, use the **File, Open** command, or click the 'file open' icon, and select **PROJECT 4**. On pressing <Enter>, the worksheet is displayed on the screen as shown below.

	A	B	C	D	E	F	G	H
1			*PROJECT ANALYSIS*					
2								
3		Jan	Feb	Mar	1st Quarter			
4	Income	£ 14,000.00	£ 15,000.00	£ 16,000.00	£ 45,000.00			
5	Costs:							
6	Wages	£ 2,000.00	£ 3,000.00	£ 4,000.00	£ 9,000.00			
7	Travel	£ 400.00	£ 500.00	£ 600.00	£ 1,500.00			
8	Rent	£ 300.00	£ 300.00	£ 300.00	£ 900.00			
9	Heat/Light	£ 150.00	£ 200.00	£ 130.00	£ 480.00			
10	Phone/Fax	£ 250.00	£ 300.00	£ 350.00	£ 900.00			
11	Adverts	£ 1,100.00	£ 1,200.00	£ 1,300.00	£ 3,600.00			
12	Total Costs	£ 4,200.00	£ 5,500.00	£ 6,680.00	£ 16,380.00			
13	*Profit*	£ 9,800.00	£ 9,500.00	£ 9,320.00	£ 28,620.00			
14	*Cumulative*	£ 9,800.00	£ 19,300.00	£ 28,620.00				
15								

Projec~4.xls

Sheet1 / Sheet2 / Sheet3 / Sheet4 / Sheet5 / Sheet6

Copying Sheets in a Workbook

We will now fill another three sheets behind the present one, in order to include information about ADEPT Consultants' trading during the other three quarters of the year. The easiest way of doing this is by copying the information in Sheet1, including the formatting and the entered formulae, onto the other three sheets, then edit the numerical information in these appropriately.

To simplify this operation, Excel has a facility which allows you to copy a sheet into a workbook. There are two ways of doing this: (a) with the mouse, or (b) using the menus.

With the mouse, make the sheet you want to copy the current sheet, then press the <Ctrl> key, and while keeping it pressed, point with the mouse on the Tab of Sheet1 and drag it to the right, as follows:

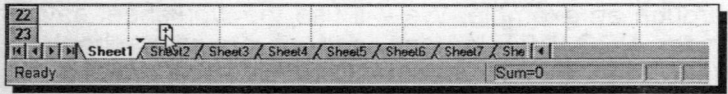

A small black triangle indicates the place where the copy will be inserted, as shown above. If you insert a copy, say before Sheet2, when you release the mouse button the inserted sheet will be given the name Sheet1(2), while inserting a second copy before Sheet2 will be given the name Sheet1(3).

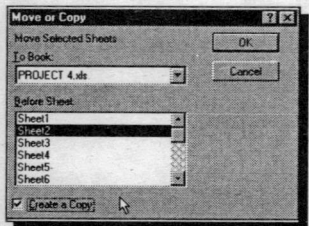

To copy a sheet with the use of menus, select the **Edit, Move or Copy Sheet** command, then highlight Sheet2 in the **Before Sheet** list of the displayed dialogue box, then check the **Create a Copy** option at the bottom of the dialogue box, and press the **OK** button. Sheet1(2) will be inserted in the Workbook, as in the above case.

When you have three copies placed, double-click the Tabs of Sheet1 and the three new sheets and change their names to 'Quarter 1', 'Quarter 2', 'Quarter 3' and 'Quarter 4', respectively.

The contents of the second sheet should be as follows:

	A	B	C	D	E	F
1	*PROJECT ANALYSIS 2nd Quarter*					
2						
3		Apr	May	Jun	2nd Quarter	
4	Income	£ 15,500.00	£ 16,000.00	£ 16,500.00	£ 48,000.00	
5	Costs:					
6	Wages	£ 3,500.00	£ 4,000.00	£ 4,500.00	£ 12,000.00	
7	Travel	£ 500.00	£ 550.00	£ 580.00	£ 1,630.00	
8	Rent	£ 300.00	£ 300.00	£ 300.00	£ 900.00	
9	Heat/Light	£ 150.00	£ 120.00	£ 100.00	£ 370.00	
10	Phone/Fax	£ 300.00	£ 350.00	£ 400.00	£ 1,050.00	
11	Adverts	£ 1,250.00	£ 1,300.00	£ 1,350.00	£ 3,900.00	
12	Total Costs	£ 6,000.00	£ 6,620.00	£ 7,230.00	£ 19,850.00	
13	*Profit*	£ 9,500.00	£ 9,380.00	£ 9,270.00	£ 28,150.00	
14	*Cumulative*	£ 9,500.00	£ 18,880.00	£ 28,150.00		
15						
16						
17						
18						

Quarter 1 \ **Quarter 2** / Quarter 3 / Quarter 4 / Sheet2

The easiest way to enter these 2nd Quarter results is to edit the copied data (from Quarter 1) by either using the EDIT key (**F2**), or double-clicking the cell you want to edit. You should now be in a position to complete editing this sheet. Be extra careful, from now on, to check the identification Tab at the bottom of the screen, so as not to get the sheets mixed up. You do not want to spend time editing the wrong worksheet!

After building up the four worksheets (one for each quarter - see page 104 at the beginning of the next chapter for details on the 3rd and 4th quarters) save the file as **PROJECT 5**.

Linking Sheets

A consolidation sheet could be placed in front of our 'stack' of data sheets to show a full year's results, by making a copy of the 1st Quarter sheet and placing it in front of it. Next, delete the entries in columns B to E, and name it 'Consolidation'.

We are now in a position to link the consolidation sheet to the other quarterly data sheets so that the information contained on them is automatically summarised and updated on it. The quarter totals in columns E of sheets Quarter 1, Quarter 2, Quarter 3, and Quarter 4, can be copied in turn to the clipboard using the **Edit, Copy** command, and then pasted to the appropriate column of the Consolidation sheet with the use of the **Edit, Paste Special** command and clicking the **Paste Link** button on the displayed dialogue box.

Note: Empty cells linked with this method, like those in cells E5 of each quarter, appear as 0 (zero) in the Consolidation sheet, and cannot be removed. To correct this, copy each column E of each quarter in two stages; E3:E4, then E6:E13.

Next, insert appropriate formulae in row 14 to correctly calculate the cumulative values in the Consolidation sheet. The result should be as follows:

E13		{='Quarter 4'!$E$6:$E$13)					
	A	B	C	D	E	F	G	H
1	*PROJECT ANALYSIS - Year Summary*							
2								
3		1st Quarter	2nd Quarter	3rd Quarter	4th Quarter			
4	Income	£ 45,000.00	£ 48,000.00	£ 52,500.00	£ 57,000.00			
5	Costs:							
6	Wages	£ 9,000.00	£ 12,000.00	£ 13,500.00	£ 15,000.00			
7	Travel	£ 1,500.00	£ 1,630.00	£ 1,930.00	£ 2,000.00			
8	Rent	£ 900.00	£ 900.00	£ 900.00	£ 900.00			
9	Heat/Light	£ 480.00	£ 370.00	£ 250.00	£ 610.00			
10	Phone/Fax	£ 900.00	£ 1,050.00	£ 1,150.00	£ 1,270.00			
11	Adverts	£ 3,600.00	£ 3,900.00	£ 4,350.00	£ 4,510.00			
12	Total Costs	£ 16,380.00	£ 19,850.00	£ 22,080.00	£ 24,290.00			
13	*Profit*	£ 28,620.00	£ 28,150.00	£ 30,420.00	£ 32,710.00			
14	*Cumulative*	£ 28,620.00	£ 56,770.00	£ 87,190.00	£119,900.00			

Finally, save the resultant workbook as **PROJECT 6**.

Linking Files

In the last example we built a consolidation report on a separate sheet in front of several parallel data sheets. All these sheets were, however, part of the same file. There may be times, however, when the consolidation data would be preferable in a separate file. As an example of linking files, we will work through an exercise to carry out this operation.

File Commands:

Use the **File, Close** command to close PROJECT6 and clear the computer's memory, and **File, Open** to open PROJECT5. Next, place another empty file in memory using the **File, New** command. You can tell that a new file has been created, because the filename Book2 appears on the Title bar.

We would like to paste links between columns E of each quarter sheet of file PROJECT 5 and the newly opened file. This is best done if both files can be viewed at the same time, so use the **Window, Arrange, Tiled** command, then copy all the labels from sheet Quarter 1 of the file PROJECT5 onto Sheet1 of the new file using the **Edit, Copy** and **Edit, Paste Special** command. The result so far should be as follows:

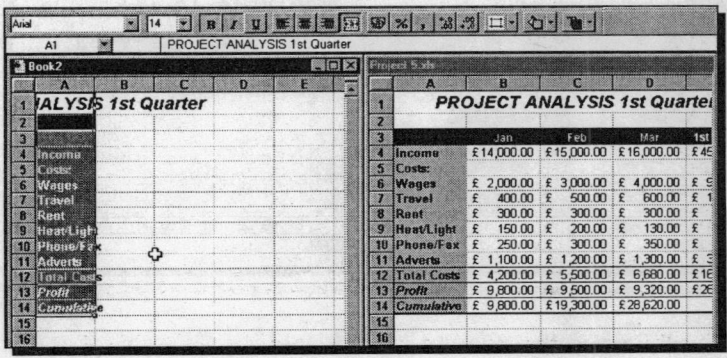

Note that the only difference between the styles of the two files is that the column widths have not transferred across when copying in this manner, therefore adjust them to a width of 11. Also the contents of cell A1 are not centred within the range A1:E1, as they should be.

Copying between files is the same as copying between the separate sheets of a file. However, here we would like to paste both the formats of the cells, and the links, therefore a two-fold copy and paste process is necessary. First, select in turn each quarter's totals from PROJECT5 (cells E3:E14 of each sheet), use the **Edit, Copy** command, and paste the formats with the **Edit, Paste Special** command, clicking the **Formats** button on the displayed dialogue box, and pressing **OK**.

Next, select each contiguous part of each quarter separately (to avoid pasting zeros where spaces should appear), copy them, and paste them with file links onto Sheet1 of the new file in columns B to E, using the **Edit, Paste Special** command and pressing the **Paste Link** button on the displayed dialogue box. Below we show this process in action when the second quarter has just been linked to Sheet1 of Book2.

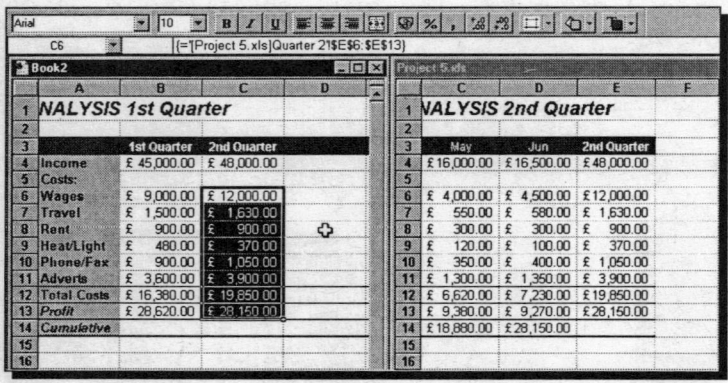

Below we show the maximised consolidated file for all four quarters.

Arial		10		B	I	U	≡ ≡ ≡			%	,					

E4		{=['Project 5.xls]Quarter 4'!$E$3:$E$4}

	A	B	C	D	E	F	G
1	**PROJECT ANALYSIS Year Summary**						
2							
3		1st Quarter	2nd Quarter	3rd Quarter	4th Quarter		
4	Income	£ 45,000.00	£ 48,000.00	£ 52,500.00	£ 57,000.00	⇩	
5	Costs:						
6	Wages	£ 9,000.00	£ 12,000.00	£ 13,500.00	£ 15,000.00		
7	Travel	£ 1,500.00	£ 1,630.00	£ 1,930.00	£ 2,000.00		
8	Rent	£ 900.00	£ 900.00	£ 900.00	£ 900.00		
9	Heat/Light	£ 480.00	£ 370.00	£ 250.00	£ 610.00		
10	Phone/Fax	£ 900.00	£ 1,050.00	£ 1,150.00	£ 1,270.00		
11	Adverts	£ 3,600.00	£ 3,900.00	£ 4,350.00	£ 4,510.00		
12	Total Costs	£ 16,380.00	£ 19,850.00	£ 22,080.00	£ 24,290.00		
13	*Profit*	£ 28,620.00	£ 28,150.00	£ 30,420.00	£ 32,710.00		
14	*Cumulative*	£ 28,620.00	£ 56,770.00	£ 87,190.00	£119,900.00		
15							

Note how cell references between different files (which could have been typed in) are shown with the filename and sheet name included in apostrophes ('...'), placed before the cell address, if the sheet name includes a space. For example

{='[PROJECT 5.XLS]Quarter 4'!$E$3:$E$4}

which implies that both files are on the drive and path.

If, however, PROJECT5 was on a different drive and, say D: and in the \DATA subdirectory, then the above formula would be given as:

{='D:\DATA\[PROJECT 5.XLS]Quarter 4'!$E$3:$E$4}

Next, add the appropriate formulae in row 14 to calculate the cumulative profits, and change the width of column E to 11.5 to accommodate the rather large year's end cumulative value. Finally, change the contents of cell A1 from 'PROJECT ANALYSIS 1st Quarter' to 'PROJECT ANALYSIS - Year Summary', before saving the linked books as **ADEPT 1**.

Relative and Absolute Cell Addresses

Entering a mathematical expression into Excel, such as the formula in cell C14 which was

   =B14+C13

causes Excel to interpret it as 'add the contents of cell one column to the left of the current position, to the contents of cell one row above the current position'. In this way, when the formula was later copied into cell address D14, the contents of the cell relative to the left position of D14 (i.e. C14) and the contents of the cell one row above it (i.e. D13) were used, instead of the original cell addresses entered in C14. This is relative addressing.

   To see the effect of relative versus absolute addressing, copy the formula in cell C14 into C17, as shown below:

C17	↓	=B17+C16			
	A	B	C	D	E	F
1	PROJECT ANALYSIS - Year Summary					
2						
3		1st Quarter	2nd Quarter	3rd Quarter	4th Quarter	
4	Income	£ 45,000.00	£ 48,000.00	£ 52,500.00	£ 57,000.00	
5	Costs:					
6	Wages	£ 9,000.00	£ 12,000.00	£ 13,500.00	£ 15,000.00	
7	Travel	£ 1,500.00	£ 1,630.00	£ 1,930.00	£ 2,000.00	
8	Rent	£ 900.00	£ 900.00	£ 900.00	£ 900.00	
9	Heat/Light	£ 480.00	£ 370.00	£ 250.00	£ 610.00	
10	Phone/Fax	£ 900.00	£ 1,050.00	£ 1,150.00	£ 1,270.00	
11	Adverts	£ 3,600.00	£ 3,900.00	£ 4,350.00	£ 4,510.00	
12	Total Costs	£ 16,380.00	£ 19,850.00	£ 22,080.00	£ 24,290.00	
13	Profit	£ 28,620.00	£ 28,150.00	£ 30,420.00	£ 32,710.00	
14	Cumulative	£ 28,620.00	£ 56,770.00	£ 87,190.00	£119,900.00	
15						
16						
17			£ -	⇩		

Note that in cell C14 the formula was =B14+C13. However, when copied into cell C17 the formula appears as

```
=B17+C16
```

because it has been interpreted as relative addressing. In this case, no value appears in cell C17 because we are attempting to add two blank cells.

Now change the formula in C14 by editing it to

```
=$B$14+$C$13
```

which is interpreted as absolute addressing. Copying this formula into cell C17 calculates the correct result. Highlight cell C17 and observe the cell references in its formula; they have not changed from those of cell C14.

The $ sign must prefix both the column reference and the row reference. Mixed cell addressing is permitted; as for example when a column address reference is needed to be taken as absolute, while a row address reference is needed to be taken as relative. In such a case, the column letter is prefixed by the $ sign.

When building an absolute cell reference in a formula, it is easier to select the cell with the mouse pointer and keep pressing the **F4** key until the correct $ prefix is set.

Freezing Panes on Screen

Sometimes there might be too much information on screen and attempting to see a certain part of a sheet might cause the labels associated with that information to scroll off the screen.

To freeze column (or row) labels on a worksheet, move the cell pointer to the right (or below) the column (or row) which you want to freeze the labels on the screen, and use the

Window, Freeze Panes

command. Everything to the left of (or above) the cell pointer will freeze on the screen.

53

In the example below, the cell pointer was placed in cell B4 of the **ADEPT 1** workbook, before issuing the command to freeze the panes. As seen on the screen dump, Excel added a vertical line between columns A and B, and a horizontal line between rows 3 and 4. Scrolling horizontally or vertically leaves column A and rows 1-3 always on screen.

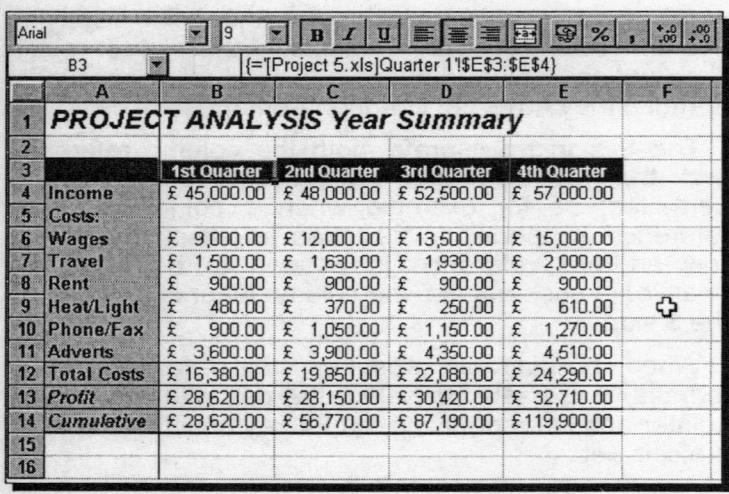

To remove unwanted frozen panes, or move their position on the worksheet, use the

Window, Unfreeze Panes

command.

5. SPREADSHEET CHARTS

Excel allows information within a worksheet to be represented in graphical form which makes data more accessible to non-expert users who might not be familiar with the spreadsheet format. The saying 'a picture is worth a thousand words', applies equally well to charts and figures.

The package allows the use of several chart and graph types, including area, bar, column, line, doughnut, radar, XY, pie, combination, and several 3-D options of these charts. In all, Excel allows fifteen different types of charts, with a total of 102 pre-defined formats, which can be selected by using the appropriate icon. These are made available to you once you have selected the data you want to chart and indicated the place you want the chart to appear on your worksheet.

Charts (you can have several per worksheet) can be displayed on screen at the same time as the worksheet from which they were derived since they appear in their own 'chart' frame and can be embedded anywhere on a worksheet. Furthermore, they can be sent to an appropriate output device, such as a plotter or printer. Although this charting module rivals a standalone graphics package, and one could write a separate book on it, an attempt will be made to present its basics, in the space available.

Preparing for a Column Chart

In order to illustrate some of the graphing capabilities of Excel, we will now plot the income of the consulting company we discussed in the **PROJECT 6** file. However, before we can go on, you will need to complete the entries for the last two quarters of trading of the Adept Consultants' example, if you haven't already done so, as follows:

	Jul	Aug	Sep	Oct	Nov	Dec
Income	17,000	17,500	18,000	18,500	19,000	19,500
Costs:						
Wages	4,000	4,500	5,000	4,500	5,000	5,500
Travel	600	650	680	630	670	700
Rent	300	300	300	300	300	300
Heat/Light	50	80	120	160	200	250
Phone/Fax	350	380	420	400	420	450
Adverts	1,400	1,450	1,500	1,480	1,500	1,530

Next, link the quarterly totals to the consolidation sheet and calculate the year's total, and save as **PROJECT 7**.

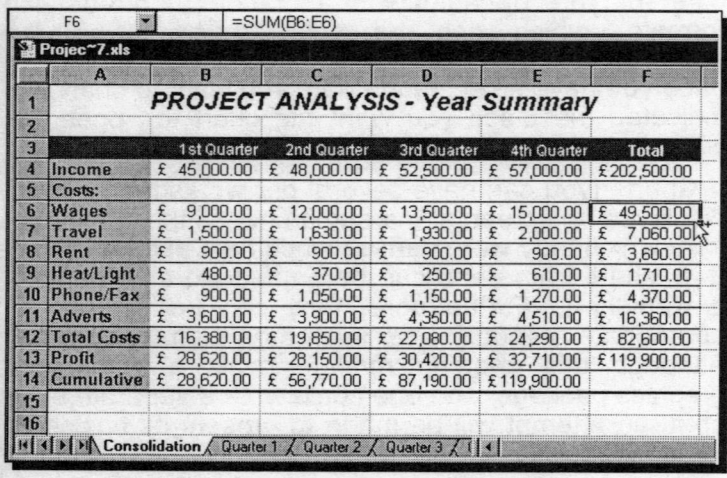

Now we need to select the range of the data we want to graph. The range of data to be graphed in Excel does not have to be contiguous for each graph, as with some other spreadsheets. With Excel, you select your data from different parts of a sheet with the <Ctrl> key pressed down. This method has the advantage of automatic recalculation should any changes be made to the original data. You could also collect data from different sheets to one 'graphing' sheet by linking them as we did with the consolidation sheet.

If you don't want the chart to be recalculated when you do this, then you must use the **Edit, Copy** and **Edit, Paste Special** commands and choose the **Values** option from the displayed dialogue box, which copies a selected range to a specified target area of the worksheet and converts formulae to values. This is necessary, as cells containing formulae cannot be pasted directly since it would cause the relative cell addresses to adjust to the new locations and each formula would then recalculate a new value for each cell and give wrong results.

The ChartWizard

To obtain a chart of 'Income' versus 'Quarters', select the data in cell range A3..E4, then either click at the ChartWizard, shown here, or use the **Insert, Chart, On This Sheet** command. Once in the worksheet area, the cursor changes to a small column chart, as shown below.

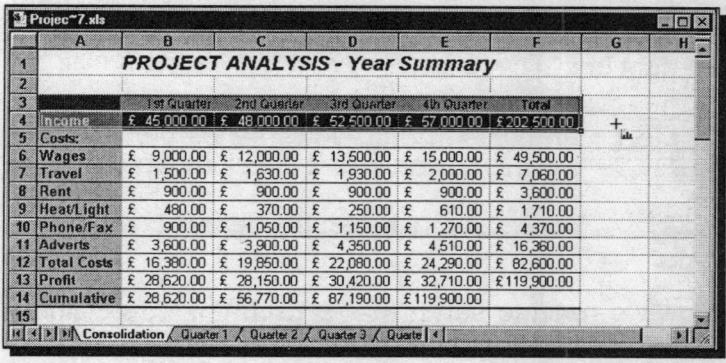

Now move the mouse pointer to the place you want to position the top-left corner of your chart, press the left mouse button and while keeping it pressed, drag the mouse down and to the right to form a dotted rectangle within which the chart will appear automatically once you release the mouse button and click the **Finish** button on the displayed ChartWizard dialogue box.

57

The result could be as follows:

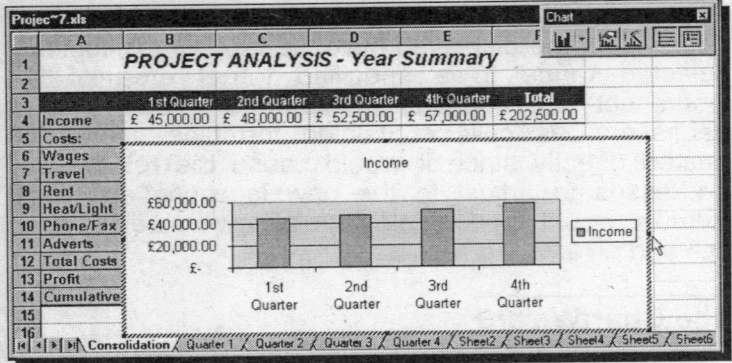

Note that while the frame containing a chart is selected (you can tell from the presence of the small black squares around it), a special Chart toolbar, shown here, appears above and to the right of it. These icons have the following function:

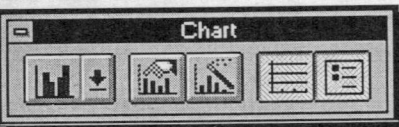

 Produces a drop-down series of icons from which you can select the chart type.

 Allows you to select the default chart.

 Allows you to select ChartWizard's dialogue boxes to specify the data range for the chart and whether the data series is in rows or columns.

 Toggles the horizontal gridlines on or off.

 Toggles the legends on or off.

You can change the size of a selected chart by dragging the small four-headed arrow pointer (which appears when the mouse pointer is placed at the edges of the frame and on the small black boxes). You can also move the whole frame to a new position by clicking within it and dragging it to its new position.

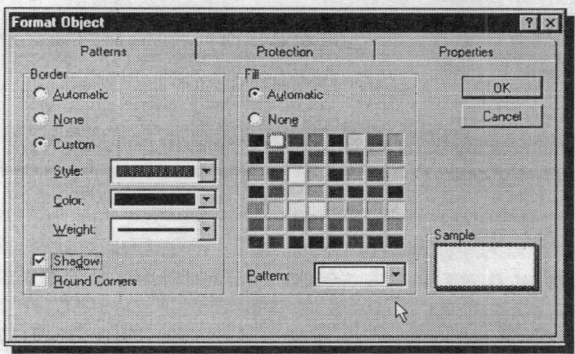

As an example of what you can do with a chart, let us select a pattern to be used as a frame, by using the **Format, Object** command and in the displayed Format Object dialogue box, shown above, select **Custom** under the Patterns tab and choose the 7th **Style**, the 4th **Weight** line, check the **Shadow** box and press **OK**. Next, click the Chart Type icon and select a 3D column chart, to obtain the displayed chart overleaf.

Try it, then change the first quarter income from £45,000 to £55,000 (on the Quarter 1 sheet), and watch how the change is reflected on the redrawn graph on the Consolidation sheet displayed on the next page.

Finally, revert to the original entry for the first quarter's income, change your chart back to a simple column type, and then save your work again under the filename **PROJECT 7** by simply pressing the Save icon shown here. Your current work will be saved to disc replacing the previous version under the same filename.

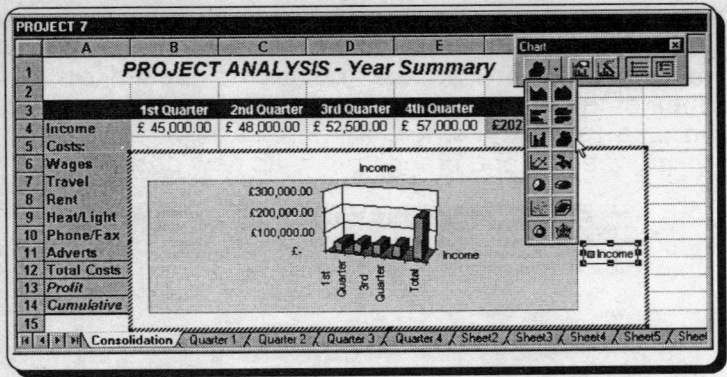

When Excel creates a chart, it plots each row or column of data in the selected range as a 'data series', such as a group of bars, lines, etc. A chart can contain many data series, but Excel charts data according to the following rules:

1.   If the selected range contains more rows than columns of data, Excel plots the data series by columns.

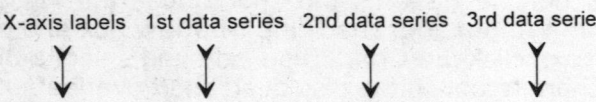

2.   If the selected range contains more columns than rows of data, or the same number of columns and rows, Excel plots the data series by rows.

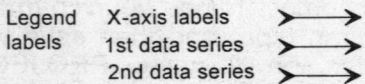

If you select a range to chart which includes column and row headings, and text above or to the left of the numeric data, Excel uses the text to create the axis labels, legends, and title.

If your data selection does not obey these rules, you must use the ChartWizard, and tell Excel how your data series is structured in the 4th displayed dialogue box. The ChartWizard opens 5 dialogue boxes altogether, as follows:

1. Range selection

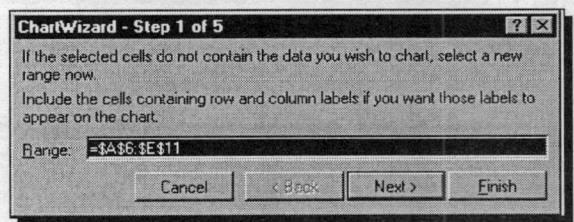

2. Chart type selection

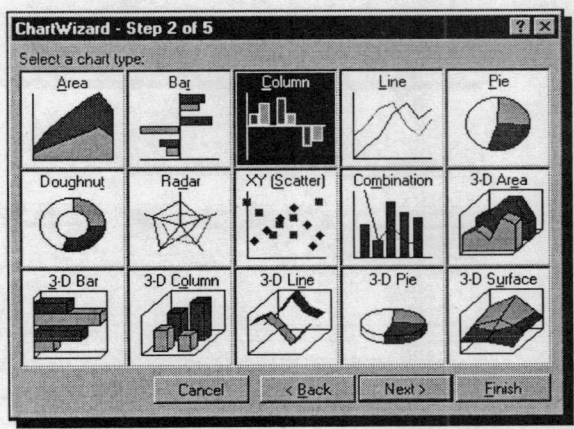

3. Format selection for chosen chart

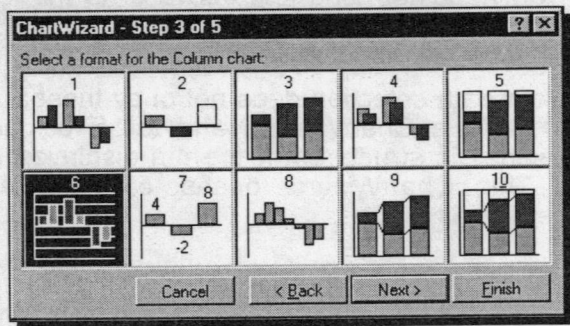

4. Data series specification

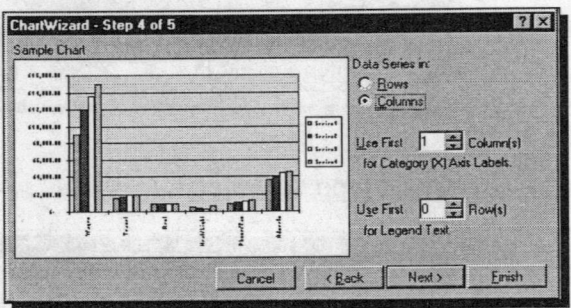

5. Legend and title selection

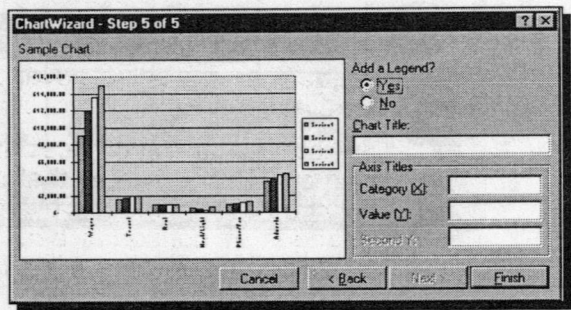

Saving and Naming Charts:

When you save a workbook, the chart or charts you have created are saved with it. Charts are numbered automatically as you create them and are given the default name **Chart #**, where **#** is a sequential number starting with 1. If you have created a chart and subsequently deleted it, the next chart created will be named one number above the deleted chart.

If you prefer, you can rename charts so that they have names more relevant to what they represent. To do so, select the chart by clicking within its boundaries, then click the Reference Indicator (above column A, which should display the name **Chart #**), type a new name and press <Enter>.

As we will be creating quite a number of charts, rename the existing **Chart 1** to **Income Bar**.

Pre-defined Chart Types

To select a different type of chart, click the ChartWizard icon shown here, or select the **Insert, Chart** command. The 2nd ChartWizard dialogue box displayed previously, lists 15 different chart options, but 6 of these are 3D versions of Area, Bar, Column, Line, Pie, and Surface charts. The nine main graph-types are normally used to describe the following relationships between data:

Area: for showing a volume relationship between two series, such as production or sales, over a given length of time.

Bar: for comparing differences in data - non-continuous data that are not related over time - by depicting changes in horizontal bars to show positive and negative variations from a given position.

Column: for comparing separate items - non-continuous data which are related over time - by depicting changes in vertical bars to show positive and negative variations from a given position.

Line: for showing continuous changes in data with time.

Pie: for comparing parts with the whole. You can use this type of chart when you want to compare the percentage of an item from a single series of data with the whole series.

Doughnut: for comparing parts with the whole. Similar to pie charts, but can depict more than one series of data.

Radar: for plotting one series of data as angle values defined in radians, against one or more series defined in terms of a radius.

XY: for showing scatter relationships between X and Y. Scatter charts are used to depict items which are not related over time.

Combination: for comparing different chart types or different scaling systems by overlaying different type of charts (up to a maximum of four).

You can change the type of chart by selecting one of the fifteen alternate chart types (including the 3D variations of Area, Bar, Column, Line, Pie, and Surface) from the 2nd ChartWizard dialogue box, pressing the **Next** button and choosing one of the pre-defined charts from the displayed selection, provided your data fits the selection.

Customising a Chart

In order to customise a chart, you need to know how to add legends, titles, text labels, arrows, and how to change the colour and pattern of the chart background, plot areas and chart markers, and how to select, move and size chart objects.

Drawing a Multiple Column Chart:

As an exercise, we will consider a new column chart which deals with the quarterly 'Costs' of Adept Consultants. To achieve this, first select the cell range A3:E3 then, while holding the <Ctrl> key down, select the costs range A6:E11, press the ChartWizard icon (or use the **Insert, Chart** command), and select the target area. The column chart of the 6 different quarterly costs will be drawn automatically, as displayed in the 4th ChartWizard dialogue box shown in the composite screen dump below. Note that the highlighting of the selected range actually disappears once the target area is defined.

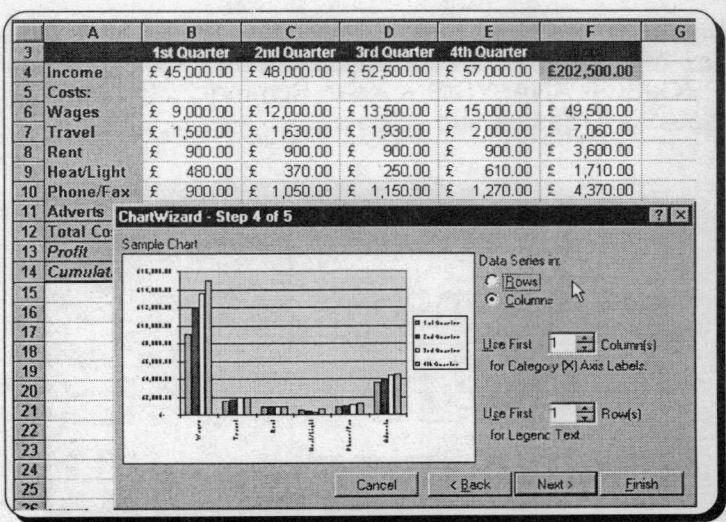

Because the selected range contains more rows than columns of data, Excel follows the 1st rule of data series selection which, however, might not be what you want.

To have the 'quarters' appearing on the x-axis and the 'costs' as the legends, we need to tell Excel that our data series is in rows by clicking the **Rows** button on the 4th ChartWizard dialogue box. Immediately this is done the column chart changes to:

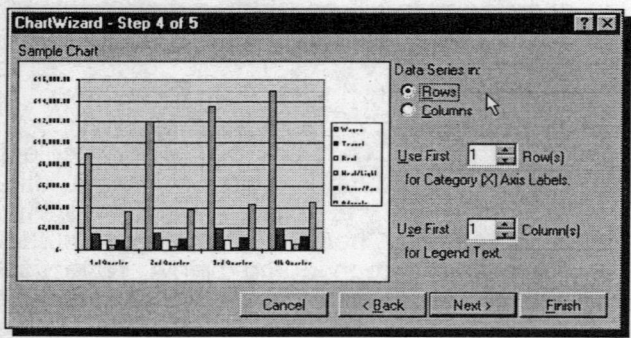

Now click the **Next** button, and type in the **Chart Title** box of the 5th ChartWizard dialogue box the heading 'PROJECT ANALYSIS - Year Summary', followed by the **Axis Titles** as shown below.

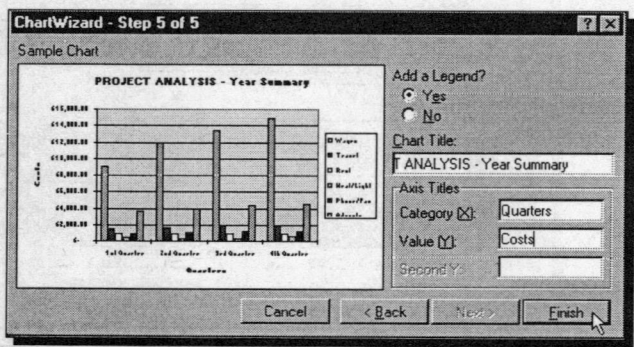

When you click the **Finish** button, the following chart appears on the screen:

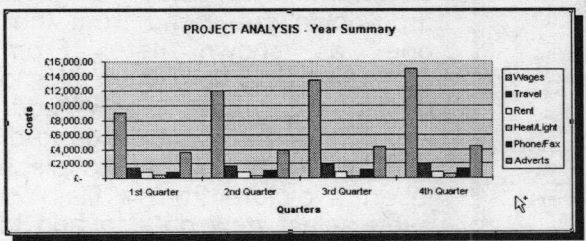

If you make a mistake and you want to try again, make sure the unwanted chart is selected, then press the <Del> key. Once you are satisfied with your efforts, name your chart **Costs Bar** and save your work under the filename **PROJECT 8**.

Changing a Title and an Axis Label:

To change a title or an axis label within a chart, double-click inside the chart. Once this is done, clicking at the title, the X- or Y-axis label, or the legends, reveals that these are individual objects (they are surrounded by small black squares) and you can edit or re-position them, or change their font and point size, as shown below.

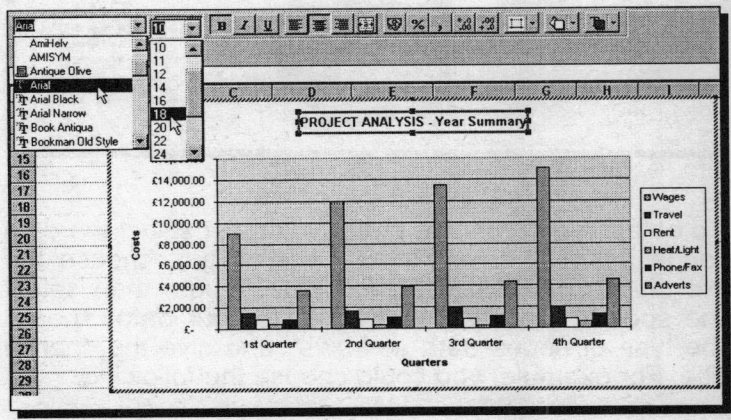

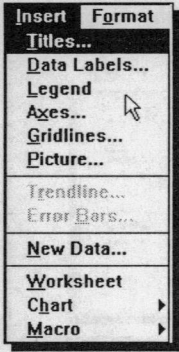

Once you have selected a chart, by double-clicking inside it, the **Insert** command reveals a changed drop-down sub-menu from the usual one, as shown here. From this sub-menu you can enter titles or axis labels, enter data labels, add chart legends, specify which axis to display, specify which gridlines to display, or insert a picture from a file. You can even select new data to add to your chart.

Drawing a Pie Chart:

To change the chart type, simply select the chart, then click the Chart Type icon on the **Chart** Toolbar and choose the pie picture from the displayed drop-down list. If the selected chart was the 'quarterly costs' chart, then on pressing the **OK** button the chart would be redrawn to the following:

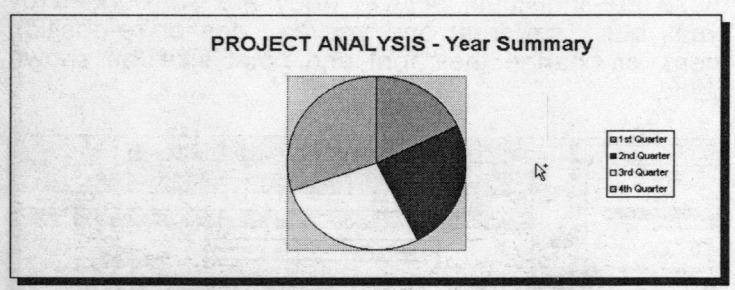

To obtain a different pie chart, you must select the data range again, then click the ChartWizard, choose the pie chart from the displayed chart types, then select the specific pie chart that best fits your data, specify the type of series data as 'rows', and give the chart a title. For example, you could choose the following:

68

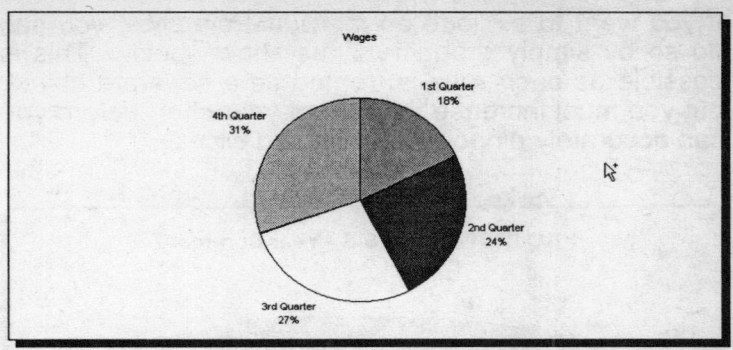

This chart tells us that Wages have increased from 18% for the 1st quarter to 31% for the 4th quarter, in a clockwise manner, but it doesn't tell us much more.

As a last example in chart drawing, we will use the data range A6:A11 and F6:F11 of the worksheet to plot a 3-D pie chart. The steps are the same as before, but for the 3-D option and specifying the type of series data as 'columns'. The result should be as follows:

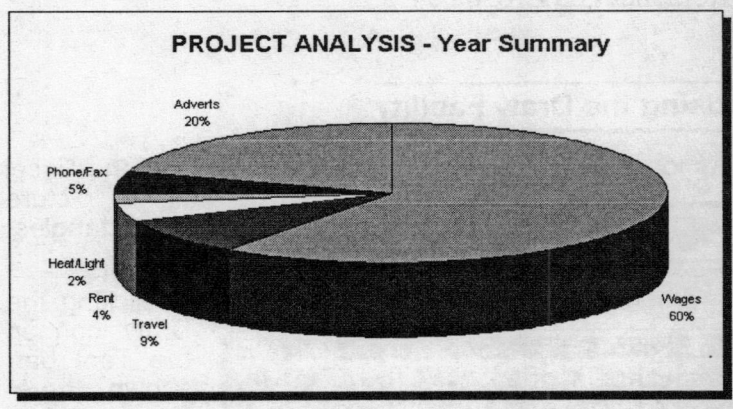

It is now obvious that the information contained in this chart is much more than in the 2-D version.

If you want to explode an individual pie slice, you can do so by simply dragging it, as shown below. This is possible as each slice is treated as a separate object, but you must increase the size of your chart before you can accurately pinpoint the required slice.

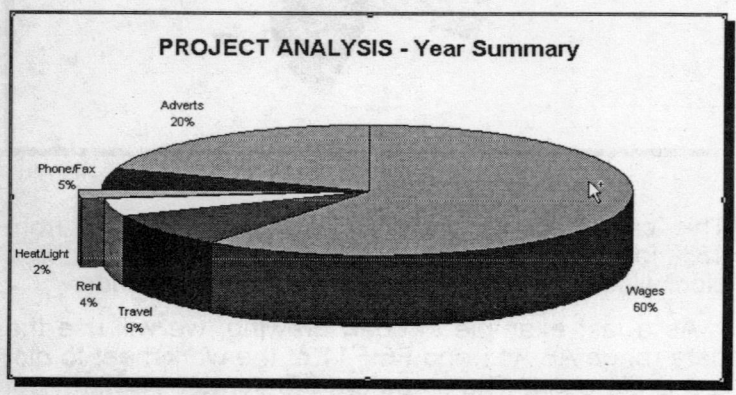

PROJECT ANALYSIS - Year Summary

Adverts 20%
Phone/Fax 5%
Heat/Light 2%
Rent 4%
Travel 9%
Wages 60%

Finally, name the pie chart **Costs Pie** and save your worksheet as **PROJECT 9**.

Using the Draw Facility

As long as you have a mouse, you can use the Excel Draw facility to create, or edit, a picture consisting of lines, arcs, ellipses, rectangles, and even text boxes.

When you activate the draw facility by clicking the

Draw icon on the Tool bar, shown here, Excel displays a new set of icons on the top left side of your workspace as shown here. These can be moved to form a 3rd Tool bar.

The Drawing icons allow you to carry out the following tasks:

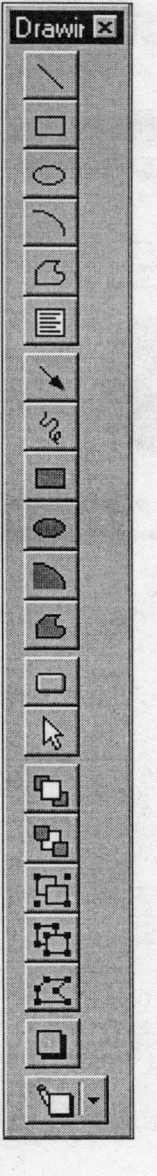

Draw a line

Draw a rectangle

Draw an ellipse

Draw an arc

Draw in freeform

Draw a text box

Draw an arrow

Draw freehand

Draw a filled rectangle

Draw a filled ellipse

Draw a filled arc

Draw a filled freeform

Create a button

Make a drawing selection

Bring an object to front

Send an object to back

Group objects

Ungroup objects

Reshape objects

Include a drop shadow

Select a pattern

The effects of these drawing tools can be superimposed on either the worksheet area or the chart area. The result is that you can annotate a worksheet to your total satisfaction, as shown below:

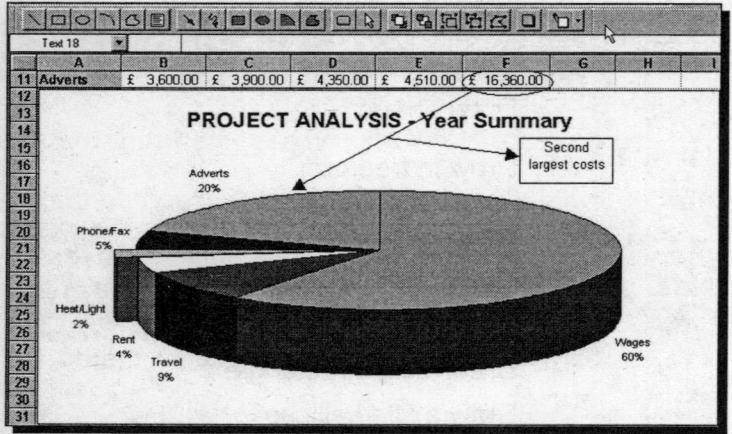

In the screen dump above, the drawing icons were moved to the top of the page, to form a 3rd Tool bar, out of the drawing area.

6. THE EXCEL DATABASE

An Excel database table is a worksheet range which contains related information, such as 'Customer's Names', 'Consultancy Details', 'Invoice No.', etc. A phone book is a simple database table, stored on paper. In Excel each record is entered as a worksheet row, with the fields of each record occupying corresponding columns.

A database table is a collection of data that exists, and is organised around a specific theme or requirement. It is used for storing information so that it is quickly accessible. To make accessing the data easier, each row (or **record**), of data within a database table is structured in the same fashion, i.e. each record will have the same number of columns (or **fields**).

We define a database and its various elements as follows:

Database table   A collection of related data organised in rows and columns in a worksheet file. A worksheet file can contain many different database tables.

Record   A row of information relating to a single entry and comprising one or more fields.

Field   A single column of information of the same type, such as people's names.

Creating a Database

In order to investigate the various database functions, such as sorting, searching, etc., we first need to set up a database table in the form shown overleaf.

Note that in creating a database table, the following rules must be observed:

1. The top row of the database table must contain the field labels, one per column, which identify the fields in the database table. The second and subsequent rows of such a database table must contain records; no blank rows should be inserted between the field labels and the records.

2. Field labels must be unique within a given database table.

3. Entries under each field must be of the same type.

4. A database table can contain a maximum of 256 fields and 16,384 records.

We assume that the 'Invoice Analysis' of Adept Consultants is designed and set out as shown below with the listed field titles and field widths. Formatting information is given below. To see all the rows of this database on your screen at once, either select the **View, Zoom** command and set the zoom level to 90%, or toggle off the **Formula Bar, Status Bar**, and only show the **Standard** and **Formatting Toolbars**.

	A	B	C	D	E	F	G
1		INVOICE ANALYSIS: ADEPT CONSULTANTS LTD AT					23/06/96
2							
3	NAME	DETAILS	No.	ISSUED	PAID?	VALUE	
4	VORTEX Co. Ltd	Wind Tunnel Tests	96001	10/01/96	N	£120.84	
5	AVON Construction	Adhesive Tests	96002	14/01/96	Y	£103.52	
6	BARROWS Associates	Tunnel Design Tests	96003	20/01/96	N	£99.32	
7	STONEAGE Ltd	Carbon Dating Tests	96004	05/02/96	N	£55.98	
8	PARKWAY Gravel	Material Size Tests (XX)	96005	11/02/96	N	£180.22	
9	WESTWOOD Ltd	Load Bearing Tests	96006	25/02/96	N	£68.52	
10	GLOWORM Ltd	Luminescence Tests	96007	10/03/96	N	£111.55	
11	SILVERSMITH Co	X-Ray Diffraction Test	96008	20/03/96	Y	£123.45	
12	WORMGLAZE Ltd	Heat Transfer Tests	96009	30/03/96	N	£35.87	
13	EALING Engines Design	Vibration Tests	96010	05/04/96	N	£58.95	
14	HIRE Service Equipment	Network Implementation	96011	15/04/96	N	£290.00	
15	EUROBASE Co. Ltd	Project Control	96012	22/04/96	N	£150.00	
16	FREEMARKET Dealers	Stock Control Package	96013	03/05/96	N	£560.00	
17	OILRIG Construct.	Metal Fatigue Tests	96014	12/05/96	N	£96.63	
18	TIME & Motion Ltd	Systems Analysis	96015	26/05/96	N	£120.35	
19	AVON Construction	Cement Fatigue Tests	96016	07/06/96	N	£111.89	
20	PARKWAY Gravel	Material Size Tests (ZZ)	96017	15/06/96	N	£190.35	
21							

Use the **Format, Column, Width** command (or use the mouse to drag the vertical separators of the column borders) to change the width of the various columns to those given below, and then enter the abbreviated titles, centrally positioned, in row 3, as shown in the worksheet on the previous page. These widths were chosen so that the whole worksheet could be seen on the screen at once.

Column	Title	Width	Type
A	NAME	21	Default or Text
B	DETAILS	20	Default or Text
C	No.	6	Custom, 0
D	ISSUED	9	Custom, dd/mm/yy
E	PAID?	7	Default or Text
F	VALUE	8	Currency

The formatting type was selected by using the **Format, Cells** command to display the dialogue box below.

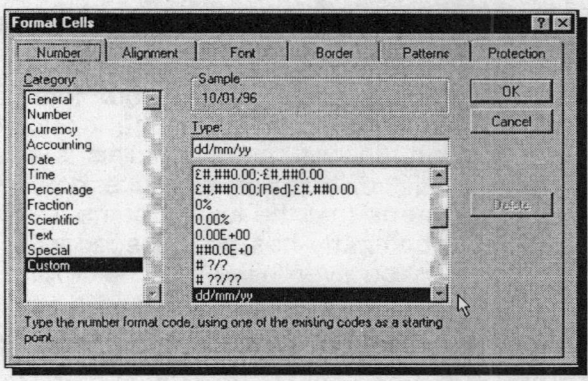

This dialogue box was used to format column C to a **Custom** category format (type 0), column D to a **Custom** category format (type dd/mm/yy), and column F to a **Currency** format, before entering the numeric information. Finally, save the worksheet under the filename **INVOICE 1**.

Sorting a Database List:

The records within our database list are in the order in which they were entered, with the 'Invoice No' shown in ascending order. However, we might find it easier to browse through the information if it was sorted in alphabetical order of 'Customer's Name'. Excel has an easy way to do this.

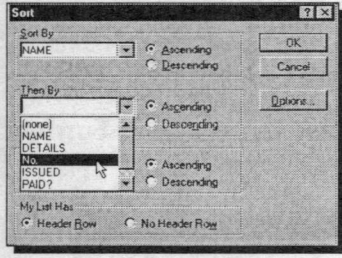

To use it, highlight the database list (data range A4:F20; don't include the field names in the range to be sorted) and, either press the 'Sort Ascending' button, shown here, or select the

Data, Sort

command, and choose in the **Sort By** list of the Sort dialogue box the name of the field on which you want to sort the database (in this case NAME). This will be the primary sort key.

The second method of sorting allows you more control over the sorting options, such as the choice of a secondary sort key (in this case No.). This is selected in the **Then By** list of the Sort dialogue box, shown above, which ensures that the lowest number invoices appear first, if a company has been issued with more than one invoice. You even have the choice of a third sort key, if you needed one.

Pressing the **OK** button produces the display shown on the next page.

The easiest way to return the database to its original sort order is either by selecting the **Edit, Undo Sort** command or by re-sorting the database in ascending order of invoice No.

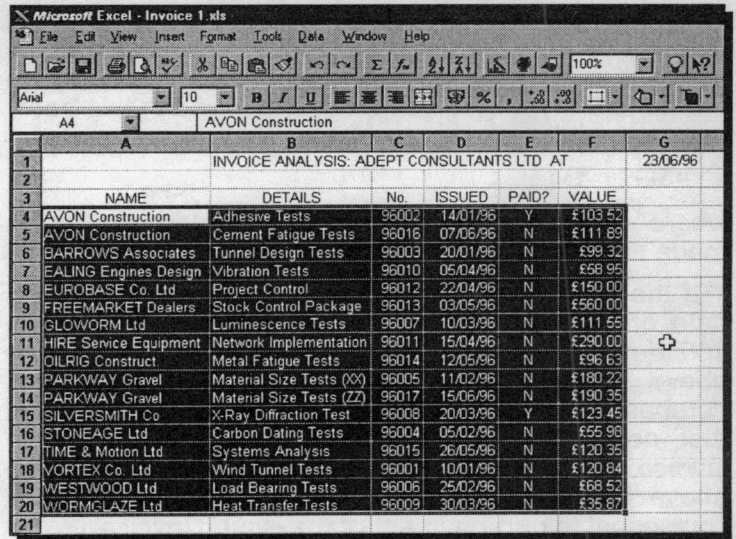

	A	B	C	D	E	F	G
1		INVOICE ANALYSIS: ADEPT CONSULTANTS LTD AT					23/06/96
2							
3	NAME	DETAILS	No.	ISSUED	PAID?	VALUE	
4	AVON Construction	Adhesive Tests	96002	14/01/96	Y	£103.52	
5	AVON Construction	Cement Fatigue Tests	96016	07/06/96	N	£111.89	
6	BARROWS Associates	Tunnel Design Tests	96003	20/01/96	N	£99.32	
7	EALING Engines Design	Vibration Tests	96010	05/04/96	N	£58.95	
8	EUROBASE Co. Ltd	Project Control	96012	22/04/96	N	£150.00	
9	FREEMARKET Dealers	Stock Control Package	96013	03/05/96	N	£560.00	
10	GLOWORM Ltd	Luminescence Tests	96007	10/03/96	N	£111.55	
11	HIRE Service Equipment	Network Implementation	96011	15/04/96	N	£290.00	
12	OILRIG Construct.	Metal Fatigue Tests	96014	12/05/96	N	£96.63	
13	PARKWAY Gravel	Material Size Tests (XX)	96005	11/02/96	N	£180.22	
14	PARKWAY Gravel	Material Size Tests (ZZ)	96017	15/06/96	N	£190.35	
15	SILVERSMITH Co	X-Ray Diffraction Test	96008	20/03/96	Y	£123.45	
16	STONEAGE Ltd	Carbon Dating Tests	96004	05/02/96	N	£55.98	
17	TIME & Motion Ltd	Systems Analysis	96015	26/05/96	N	£120.35	
18	VORTEX Co. Ltd	Wind Tunnel Tests	96001	10/01/96	N	£120.84	
19	WESTWOOD Ltd	Load Bearing Tests	96006	25/02/96	N	£68.52	
20	WORMGLAZE Ltd	Heat Transfer Tests	96009	30/03/96	N	£35.87	
21							

Date Arithmetic

There are several date functions which can be used in Excel to carry out date calculations. For example, typing the function =DATE(96,6,23) returns the date 23/6/96, while the function =DATEVALUE("23/6/96"), returns the number of days since 1 January 1900. Typing the function =NOW( ), returns the current date and time as given by your computer's internal clock.

Unlike Lotus 1-2-3, with Excel you don't need to use the DATE and DATEVALUE functions when entering dates. You could, for example, write in a cell the formula:

=NOW()–D4

which allows Excel to calculate the difference in days between now and the mentioned date (**if the appropriate cell is formatted for integer numbers**) .

77

We could use this formula to work out the number of overdue days of the unpaid invoices in our example, by typing it in cell G4. However, if you want to compare the numbers you get with those displayed in this book, use instead the following formula:

=$G$1–D4

where $G$1 causes an 'absolute' reference to be made to the contents of cell G1.

If the record in row 4 of the worksheet refers to the data of VORTEX Co. Ltd., then the result should be 165 days. However, before we proceed to copy the above formula to the rest of the G column of the database list, we should take into consideration the fact that, normally, such information is not necessary if an invoice has been paid. Therefore, we need to edit the above formula in such a way as to make the result conditional to non-payment of the issued invoice.

The IF Function

The IF function allows comparison between two values with the use of special 'logical' operators. The logical operators we can use are listed below.

Logical	operators
=	Equal to
<	Less than
>	Greater than
<=	Less than or Equal to
>=	Greater than or Equal to
<>	Not Equal to

The general format of the IF function is as follows:

IF(Comparison,Outcome-if-true,Outcome-if-false)

which contains three arguments separated by commas.

78

The first argument of the IF function is the 'logical comparison', the second is what should happen if the outcome of the logical comparison is 'true', while the third is what should happen if the outcome of the logical comparison is 'false'.

Thus, we can incorporate the IF function in the formula we entered in cell G4 to calculate the days overdue only if the invoice has not been paid, otherwise the string 'N/A' should be written into the appropriate cell, should the contents of the corresponding E column of a record be anything else but N. Either edit the formula in cell G4, by double-clicking the cell, or retype it. The final version of the formula in cell G4 should now correspond to what is shown below.

    =IF(E4="N",$G$1–D4," N/A")

Now copy this formula to the rest of the appropriate range (G5:G20) and compare your results with those shown below.

	A	B	C	D	E	F	G	H
1		INVOICE ANALYSIS: ADEPT CONSULTANTS LTD AT					23/06/96	
2								
3	NAME	DETAILS	No.	ISSUED	PAID?	VALUE	OVERDUE	
4	VORTEX Co. Ltd	Wind Tunnel Tests	96001	10/01/96	N	£120.84	165	
5	AVON Construction	Adhesive Tests	96002	14/01/96	Y	£103.52	N/A	
6	BARROWS Associates	Tunnel Design Tests	96003	20/01/96	N	£99.32	155	
7	STONEAGE Ltd	Carbon Dating Tests	96004	05/02/96	N	£55.98	139	
8	PARKWAY Gravel	Material Size Tests (XX)	96005	11/02/96	N	£180.22	133	
9	WESTWOOD Ltd	Load Bearing Tests	96006	25/02/96	N	£68.52	119	
10	GLOWORM Ltd	Luminescence Tests	96007	10/03/96	N	£111.55	105	
11	SILVERSMITH Co	X-Ray Diffraction Test	96008	20/03/96	Y	£123.45	N/A	
12	WORMGLAZE Ltd	Heat Transfer Tests	96009	30/03/96	N	£35.87	85	
13	EALING Engines Design	Vibration Tests	96010	05/04/96	N	£58.95	79	
14	HIRE Service Equipment	Network Implementation	96011	15/04/96	N	£290.00	69	
15	EUROBASE Co. Ltd	Project Control	96012	22/04/96	N	£150.00	62	
16	FREEMARKET Dealers	Stock Control Package	96013	03/05/96	N	£560.00	51	
17	OILRIG Construct.	Metal Fatigue Tests	96014	12/05/96	N	£96.63	42	
18	TIME & Motion Ltd	Systems Analysis	96015	26/05/96	N	£120.35	28	
19	AVON Construction	Cement Fatigue Tests	96016	07/06/96	N	£111.89	16	
20	PARKWAY Gravel	Material Size Tests (ZZ)	96017	15/06/96	N	£190.35	8	
21								

Your results might differ substantially from the ones shown above, if you have used the NOW( ) function in cell G1. After checking your work, save it under the filename **INVOICE 2**.

Searching a Database

A database can be searched for specific records that meet certain criteria. We will use the database of worksheet **INVOICE 2** to illustrate the method.

Assuming that the database is on your screen, we need only place the cell pointer within the data list (we put it on cell A4, although anywhere within the range A4:G20 would do), for Excel to instinctively know the range of your data.

Using the Database Form:

After the cell pointer is placed within the database list, Excel creates automatically a database form, as shown below, which is accessed by selecting the **Data, Form** command. The database form can be used to add, delete, edit, and search for specific records.

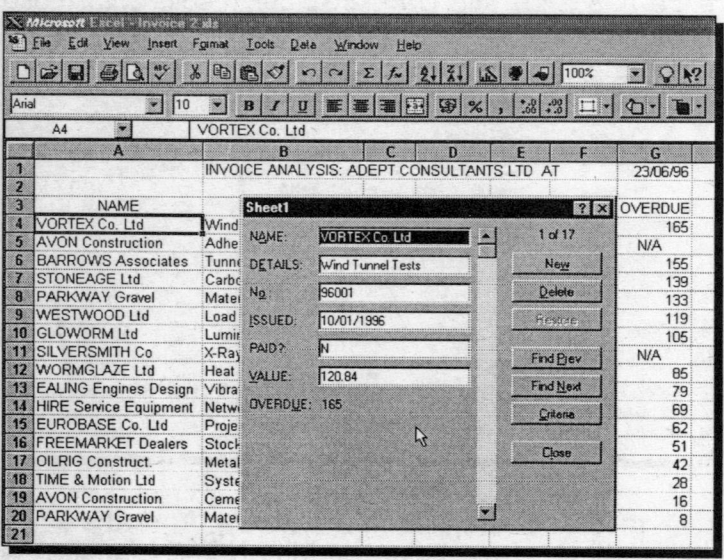

Note that the field names at the top row of the database appear on the left side of the form. On the top right corner of the form (above the **New** button) the entry '1 of 17' is displayed to indicate that this is the first of 17 records.

Most of the field names within the database form have one letter underlined, which can be used to access the corresponding box in the middle of the form in which the value of each field of the particular record is shown. To select fields or buttons, press the <Alt> key plus the underlined letter on field text or button, or point and click with the mouse. To move the highlighter forward through fields and buttons press the <Tab> key, while to move backwards, press <Shift+Tab>.

With the help of the database form, adding new records is made easy. On pressing the **New** button, an empty form is displayed for you to fill in. Editing a displayed record is even easier; that is why the **Restore** button is included. The function of the form buttons is as follows:

Button	*Function*
New	Clears the field entries in the displayed form so that new information can be added. Pressing **New** again, adds the data just typed as a new record in the database.
Delete	Deletes the displayed record and shifts the remaining records one up the list. A deleted record cannot be restored. If you delete a record accidentally, re-open the database file without saving the changes.
Restore	Restores edited fields in the displayed record, removing the changes just made. Entries must be restored before pressing <Enter> or scrolling to another record.

Find **Prev**	Displays the previous record in the list. If criteria have been selected, then pressing **Find** **Prev** displays the previous record that matches the criteria.
Find **Next**	Displays the nest record in the list. If criteria have been selected, then pressing **Find Next** displays the next record that matches the criteria.
Criteria	Displays a dialogue box in which you can enter comparison criteria with comparison operators to find records that meet these restrictions.
C**l**ose	Closes the data form.
C**l**ear	Available after pressing the **Criteria** button. It removes existing criteria from the Criteria dialogue box.
Form	Available after pressing the **Criteria** button. It returns you to the default data form.

Finding Records:

There are two ways of finding specific records from within a database. The first method involves the use of the database form, while the second method involves the filtering of data by using a criteria range within the worksheet to display only the rows that meet all the specified criteria.

Excel's database form can be used to find records provided the records we are looking for meet simple criteria. To enter the criteria, press the **Criteria** button on the database form which will cause a blank form to be displayed, with the cursor blinking in the first field. Now move to the 'PAID' field and type N, then to the 'VALUE' field and type >150, as shown on the next page.

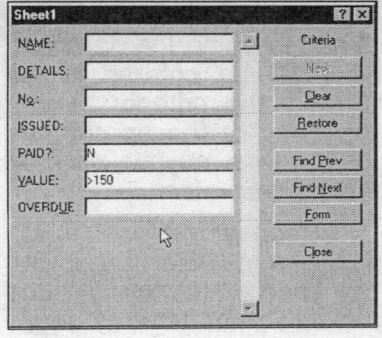

On pressing the **Find Next** button, the first record that meets both these criteria is displayed - in this case, the 5th record (PARKWAY Gravel). Pressing the **Find Next** button again three more times, displays the 11th, 13th and 17th record in succession.

To use Excel's second method for finding and extracting data, we need to specify an area of the worksheet for setting our criteria for the search. To do this, first copy the field names of the database (A3:G3) to an empty area of the worksheet, say, A23:G23 which will form the first line of the 'criteria range'. Label this area CRITERIA FOR SEARCHING in cell A22.

Now type in cells E24 and F24 the actual criteria which is N and >150, respectively, then use the **Data, Filter, Advanced Filter** command and specify in the displayed dialogue box the **List Range** and **Criteria Range** as A3:G20 and A23:G24 (it includes the field names in both cases). On pressing the **OK** button, Excel filters the data **In-Place** by hiding the rows that do not meet the criteria, as shown below.

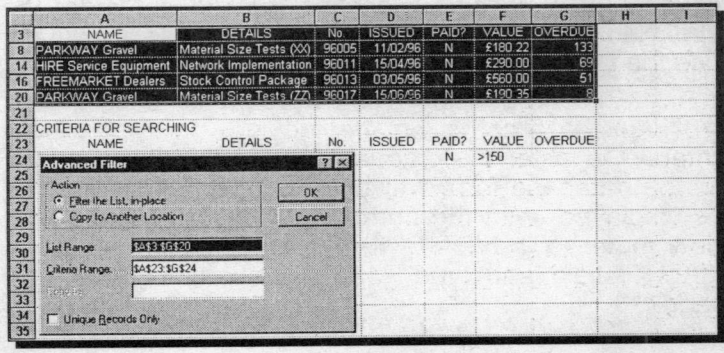

83

Do not specify an empty line as part of the criterion range, as this has the effect of searching the database for **all** records. The criteria must be entered in the second and subsequent rows of the criterion range, with each entered below the copy of the appropriate field name. A label (text) or a value may be entered exactly as it appears in the database.

In the case of searching a database for label (text), such as under the fields 'NAME' and 'DETAILS' in our example, you can use the two special characters ? and * (known as 'wildcard characters') to match any single character of a label or all characters to the end of the label.

To search a database for values, either enter the value as the exact criterion or use a simple numeric comparison, such as >90, in which the logical operators (<, <=, >, >=, <>) can be used. The logical formula generates a value of 1 if the condition is TRUE or a value of 0 if the condition is FALSE.

Several criteria can be entered, either in the same row, if you want Excel to search for records that match every criterion (i.e. criteria entered are linked with the logical AND), or one per row, if you want Excel to search records that satisfy any of the criteria (i.e. criteria entered are linked with the logical OR).

As seen above, selecting the **Filter the List, in-place** option in the Advanced Filter dialogue box, causes Excel to hide the rows that do not meet the specified criteria. To see the full database list again, use the **Data, Filter, Show All** command.

Extracting Records

To extract records and have them copied into another area of the worksheet, we need to select the **Copy to Another Location** option in the Advanced Filter dialogue box. But first, we need to set-up a second area - the 'output range'. To do this, copy the field names to the cell range A28:G28 and label it as 'OUTPUT RANGE' in cell A27, as shown below.

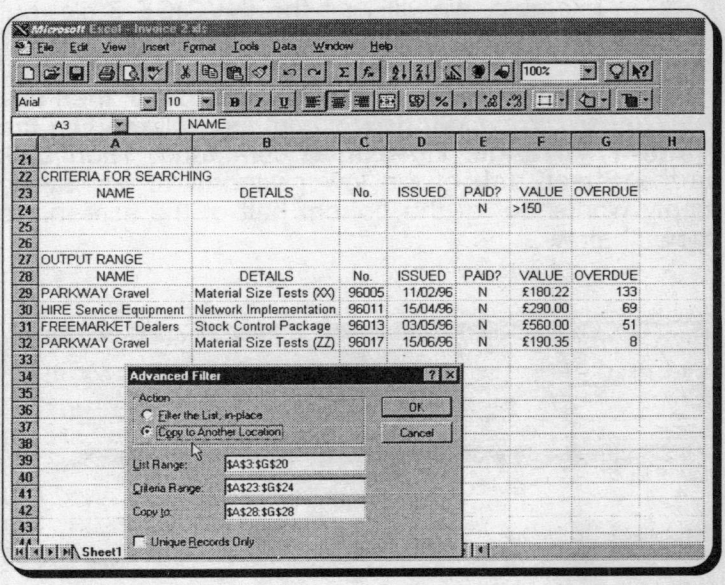

Note that we chose to put the criteria and output ranges in rows below the actual database (perhaps not the best position), rather than on the side of it. This avoids the errors that might ensue should we later decide to insert a row in our database, which will also insert a row in the criteria/output range. For a more structured worksheet layout, see end of chapter.

Save this worksheet under the filename **INVOICE 3**.

Structuring a Workbook

In a well designed worksheet, areas of calculations using formulae which we call reports, must be kept on a separate sheet from the data entry sheet. The reason for this is to prevent accidental overwriting of formulae that might be contained within the data entry sheet. Indeed, one should use a separate worksheet altogether, if so inclined.

As an example, we will use the **INVOICE 3** file, but instead of extracting data into the same sheet, we will use another sheet into which to copy the extracted records. To do this, first open file **INVOICE 3**, then use the **Window, New Window** command, followed by the **Window, Arrange, Horizontal** command. Then click on the Sheet2 tab of the lower window to display an empty worksheet at the bottom half of the screen, as shown below.

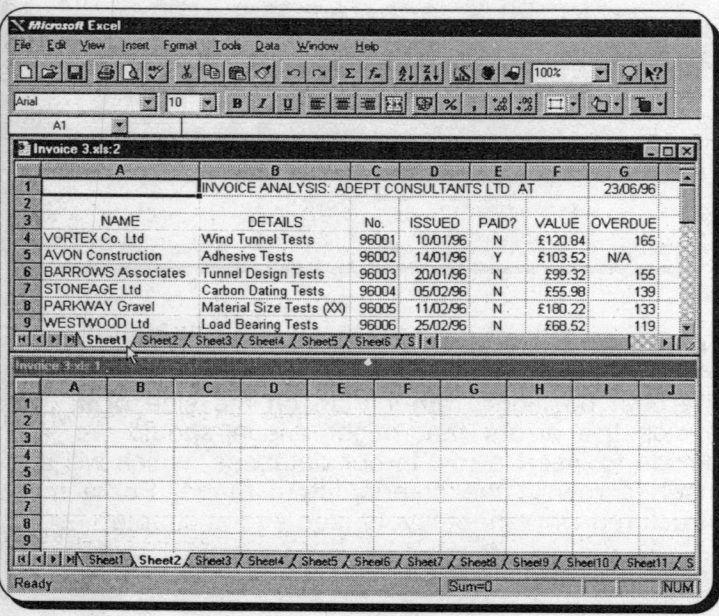

Now use the **Edit, Cut** and **Edit, Paste** commands to transfer cell range A22:G28 of Sheet1 to a range starting at cell A1 of Sheet2 and adjust the widths of the various columns to match those of Sheet1. Finally, use the **Data, Filter, Advanced Filter** command, click the **Copy to Another Location** radio button on the Advanced Filter dialogue box, and enter the information shown below.

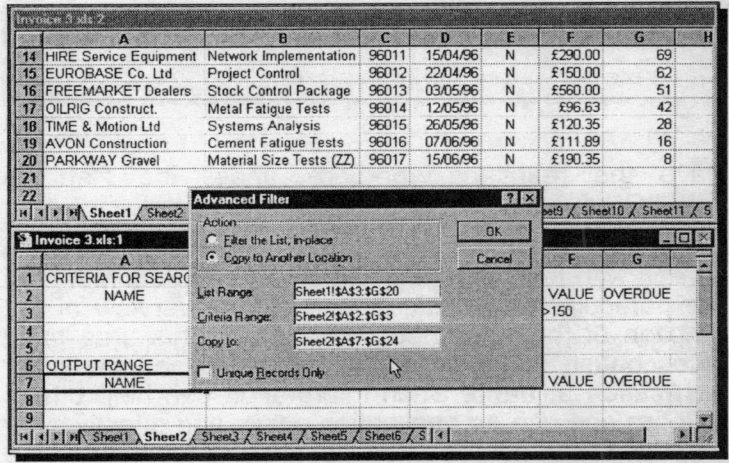

Note: Excel only extracts data into an active sheet. Therefore, you must make Sheet2 the active sheet, and since the program also requires to know which are the database field labels, place the cell pointer in cell A7, before you use the **Data, Filter, Advanced Filter** command. The address in the **List Range** box of the Advanced Filter dialogue box must be changed to indicate the correct address for the database list which is

```
Sheet1!$A$3:$G$20
```

The **Criteria Range** and the **Copy to** address locations should be prefixed with Sheet2! for correct data extraction.

Pressing the **OK** button causes the records that match the specified criteria to be extracted from Sheet1 and copied into Sheet2, as shown below.

	A	B	C	D	E	F	G
7	NAME	DETAILS	No.	ISSUED	PAID?	VALUE	OVERDUE
8	PARKWAY Gravel	Material Size Tests (XX)	96005	11/02/96	N	£180.22	133
9	HIRE Service Equipment	Network Implementation	96011	15/04/96	N	£290.00	69
10	FREEMARKET Dealers	Stock Control Package	96013	03/05/96	N	£560.00	51
11	PARKWAY Gravel	Material Size Tests (ZZ)	96017	15/06/96	N	£190.35	8
12							
13							
14							
15							

Save the resultant workbook under the filename **INVOICE 4**.

Another aspect of structuring is the provision of a screen with technical information about the contents of the particular workbook; a kind of an overview of the function of the worksheet application. This area must also contain instructions for the use of the particular application at hand. Such information can help others to learn and use an application easily and effectively. If you use range names, then include a range name table in your information screen(s).

Finally, provide a separate sheet within a workbook, or a separate worksheet altogether, for macros (the subject of the next chapter), which are in a programming language that allows you to chain together menu commands. Sensitive sheets or indeed whole workbooks can be protected using the **Tools, Protection** command and either select the **Protect Sheet** or the **Protect Workbook** option, according to your application needs, to restrict cell entries to unprotected cells. This prevents accidental changes being made to cells containing formulae.

7. USING MACROS

In Excel, you can automate tasks or create complete applications by writing macros. A macro is a sequence of commands and instructions that can control Excel.

Excel 7 for Windows 95, supports two types of macros; those written using Visual Basic - a true programming language, and those written under earlier versions of Excel using the command and/or function macro language, which in Excel 5 & 7 terminology is known as the Excel 4.0 macro language. Although the instructions of the Excel 4.0 macro language have been enhanced to accommodate all the new features of Excel 7, this macro language is only supported for backward compatibility purposes.

Understanding Visual Basic makes it easier to also program with MS-Word, MS-Project, MS-Access, and other Microsoft applications that use the language. However, for simple work you don't really have to learn to program in Visual Basic, as Excel provides you with a Macro Recorder. The Macro Recorder stores the actions you take and the commands you use while working with Excel, which can then be played back (run) to repeat the recorded actions and commands.

The Excel 7 Macro Recorder can be instructed, just as that of Excel 5, to record either in Visual Basic or in the Excel 4.0 macro language. Both of these methods will be examined, starting with the macro command language so that those who have macros written in that language can see the differences between it and Visual Basic. If you are new to Excel, then you only need to use the Visual Basic method, as this is the only programming language that Microsoft will support in the future.

Using the Macro Recorder

We will now use the worksheet saved under **PROJECT 3** (see page 38) to show how we can use Excel's Macro Recorder to create a macro to perform 'what-if' type of projections by, say, increasing the 'Wages' bill by 15%.

If you haven't saved **PROJECT 3** on disc, it will be necessary for you to enter the information shown below into Excel so that you can benefit from what is to be introduced at this point.

If you have saved **PROJECT 3**, then use the **File, Open** command to display the worksheet as shown below.

	A	B	C	D	E	F	G
1	PROJECT ANALYSIS: ADEPT CONSULTANTS LTD						
2							
3		Jan	Feb	Mar	1st Quarter		
4	Income	£ 14,000.00	£15,000.00	£ 16,000.00	£ 45,000.00		
5	Costs:						
6	Wages	£ 2,000.00	£ 3,000.00	£ 4,000.00	£ 9,000.00		
7	Travel	£ 400.00	£ 500.00	£ 600.00	£ 1,500.00		
8	Rent	£ 300.00	£ 300.00	£ 300.00	£ 900.00		
9	Heat/Light	£ 150.00	£ 200.00	£ 130.00	£ 480.00		
10	Phone/Fax	£ 250.00	£ 300.00	£ 350.00	£ 900.00		
11	Adverts	£ 1,100.00	£ 1,200.00	£ 1,300.00	£ 3,600.00		
12	Total Costs	£ 4,200.00	£ 5,500.00	£ 6,680.00	£ 16,380.00		
13	Profit	£ 9,800.00	£ 9,500.00	£ 9,320.00	£ 28,620.00		
14	Cumulative	£ 9,800.00	£19,300.00	£ 28,620.00			
15							

Project 3.xls

What we would like to do now is to edit the entries under 'Wages' so that this part of the costs can be increased by 15%. One way of doing this would be to multiply the contents of each cell containing the 'wages' value by 1.15.

To do this, we would start by changing the contents of cell B6 into a formula, by pressing the **F2** function key to 'Edit' the value in it by adding an equals sign at the beginning of the entry and then typing '*1.15' at the end of it, which has the effect of multiplying the contents of the cell by 1.15, thus increasing its contents by 15%. We would then press the <Enter> key which would cause the cell pointer to drop to B7, press the ↑ arrow key to move back to cell B6, then press the → arrow key to move to cell C6 and repeat the whole procedure. The exact steps, after highlighting cell B6, are:

Manual Procedure
Press **F2** to 'Edit' cell
Press the <Home> key to move to beginning of entry
Type = to change entry to formula
Press <End> to move to the end of the entry
Type *1.15
Press the <Enter> key
Press ↑ arrow key
Press → arrow key.

Recording an Excel 4.0 Macro:

Having opened the **PROJECT 3** file, highlight cell B6 - the first cell we want to operate on. Then, select the **Tools, Record Macro, Record New Macro** command which displays the Record New Macro dialogue box with the default **Macro Name** given as Macro1. This can be changed by you to some more meaningful name, if you so wished. Next, press the **Options** button on this dialogue box to reveal the additional dialogue box, as shown in the composite screen dump oveleaf.

In the second dialogue box we choose the **Language** and **Shortcut Key** as 'MS Excel 4.0 Macro' and 'Crtl+w', respectively.

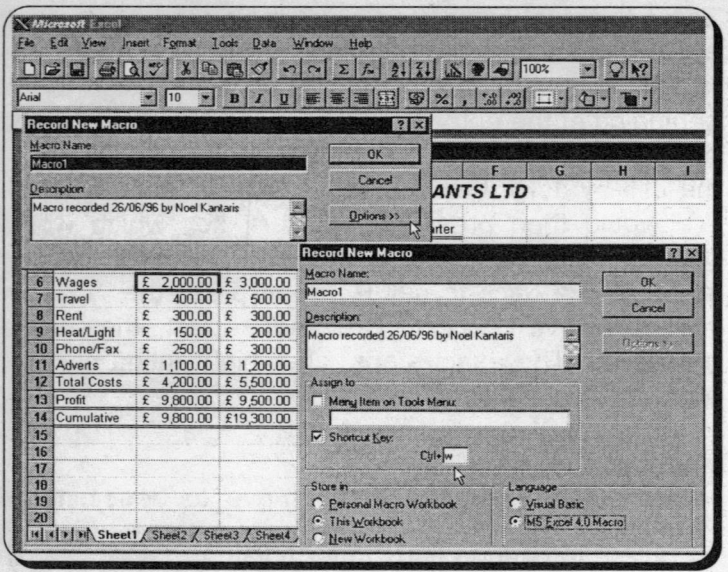

On pressing the **OK** button, Excel displays the Macro
 Stop button, shown here. Everything you type
from now on becomes part of the macro. To
start recording our macro, press/type the
appropriate key/information, as shown below.

F2
<Home>
=
<End>
*1.15
<Enter>
Press ↑ arrow key
Press → arrow key.

followed by clicking the Macro Stop button (or by
choosing **Tools, Record Macros, Stop Macros**
command).

Next, change the entry in cell B6 back to 2000, and repeat the process of recording a new macro, but this time select in the second Record New Macro dialogue box 'Visual Basic' and 'Crtl+s' for the **Language** and **Shortcut Key**, respectively.

To see both types of macros side-by-side, use the **Window, New Window** command twice, the first time highlighting the Macro1 tab (to be found beyond Sheet16), and the second time Module1 (to be found after Macro1), as shown below.

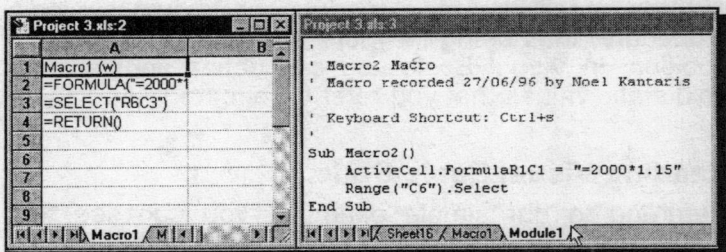

Before executing either of these macros, activate worksheet **PROJECT 3** and change the entry in cell B6 back to its original value of 2000 (it was changed by 15% while you were typing the latest macro commands), then save the macros with the worksheet, but giving your workbook the filename **AUTOPRO 1**. This is a simple precaution because, should things go wrong and your macro does unpredictable things to your worksheet, it will be easier to reopen the original worksheet than it would be to correct it!

To run the first macro, place the cell pointer on cell B6, then press **Ctrl+w**, while to run the second macro, place the cell pointer on cell B6, then press **Ctrl+s**. In both cases the shortcut key starts the appropriate macro and changes automatically the entry in B6 by 15%.

93

Programming Advantages with Visual Basic

From our simple example, the differences between the two ways of writing macros are almost indistinguishable. However, there are many advantages in using Visual Basic when the macros you write become more complicated.

In Visual Basic you can assign values directly to variables instead of storing a value in a name as you would have to do in the macro command language. Variables can be made available to all procedures, to just the procedure in a module, or to just a single procedure, thus being far more flexible than names. In addition, in Visual Basic you can define constants to hold static values that you refer to repeatedly.

Reading Visual Basic Code:

Referring to our simple example, you can see that Visual Basic has created a macro that is preceded by comment statements (that start with an apostrophe (')) in which you are informed of the name of the macro, who created it and when, and the keyboard shortcut.

The macro commands are placed in between the two keywords **Sub** and **End Sub** which mark the beginning and end of a macro. In general, keywords, variables, operators, and procedure calls are referred to as statements which are the instructions to Excel to perform some action.

The statement

```
ActiveCell.FormulaR1C1 = "=2000*1.15"
```

is the way that Visual Basic enters the formula **=2000*1.15** into the active cell. In Visual Basic terminology; it uses the **Range** object to identify the range you want to change and sets the **Formula** property of the range to assign a formula to the range.

An 'object' is something you control in Visual Basic. Each object has characteristics called 'properties' which control the appearance of the object. Objects also have 'methods' which are actions that they can take.

In Visual Basic, you use:

- Objects (such as Workbooks, Worksheets, Ranges, Charts) to perform a task. Each object has characteristics, called properties, that make that object useful by controlling the appearance or behaviour of an object.

- Properties (such as ActiveCell, ActiveSheet, Value, Selection, ColumnWidth, RowHeight), to examine the condition of an object by returning the value of one of the object's properties (such as a character string for Value, a numeric value for ColumnWidth, True, or False).

- Methods which are actions that objects can do (such as Calculate, Clear, Copy, Justify, or Table). Methods are a part of objects just like properties. The difference between them is that properties have values which are set or returned, while methods are actions you would like an object to perform.

Should you want to learn to program in Visual Basic, then may we suggest you look up the book *Programming in Visual Basic for Windows* (BP346), also published by BERNARD BABANI (publishing) Ltd.

Editing a Macro

A macro can be edited by either double-clicking in the macro window or choosing the **Tools, Macro** command, selecting the macro, and pressing the **Edit** button on the displayed dialogue box.

Since each of the three months in our worksheet is to be changed, we can replicate the first two entries of our macro (in this case Macro2), change them appropriately so that reference is made to the correct amount of wages in the **ActiveCell.Formula** command and the correct cell reference in the **Range().Select** command and insert these before the **End Sub**. This is then repeated for the last month. The complete macro is shown below.

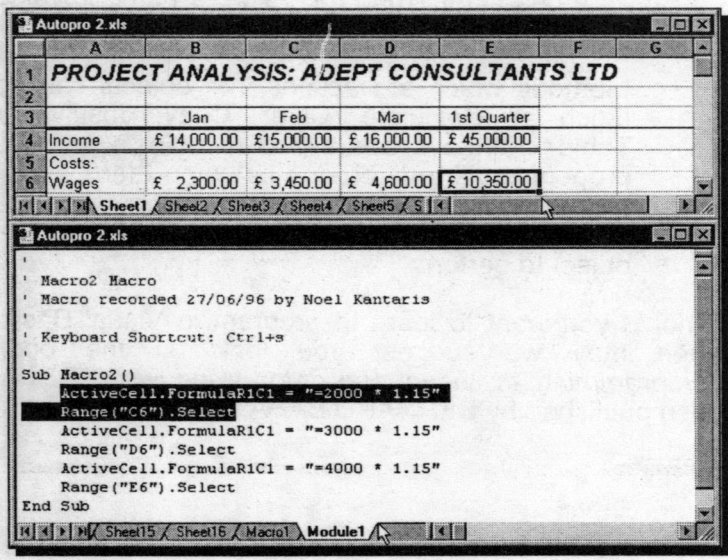

Save this workbook under the filename **AUTOPRO 2** before attempting to run the changed macro.

If your macro is correct, activating cell B6 and pressing **Ctrl+s** runs it and changes the values of the wages entries for the three months to those shown on the worksheet window on the previous page.

We could use the same macro to find out the effect of increasing wages by different percentages by editing it, but this would be rather inefficient. A better method is to allocate a cell for the % increase, say cell G5, and edit the macro so that reference to that cell is made in the R1C1 absolute format. In this example, from cell B6 we would have to refer to R[-1]C[5] (Row 1 above present position, Column 5 from present position) which is the reference to cell G5 from B6.

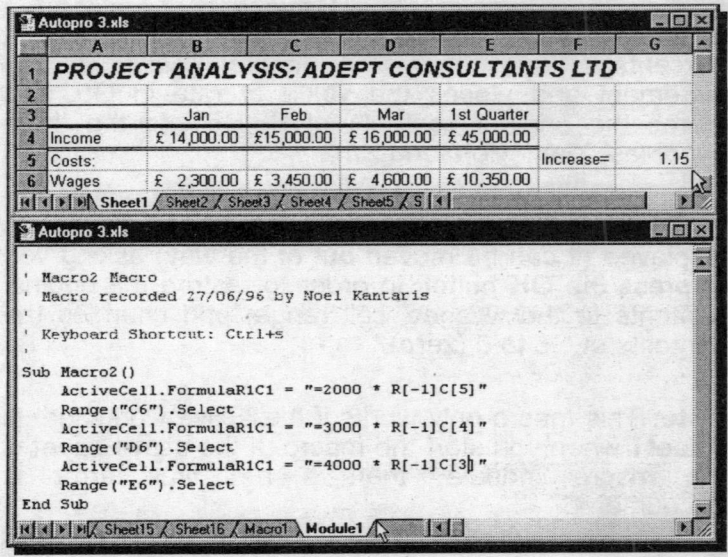

Save the newly edited Macro(3) as Module3, and the worksheet as **AUTOPRO 3**.

Macro Interaction with Keyboard:

A further addition to the above macros could be made to allow for user entry of the 'increment' value from the keyboard, rather than having to edit cell G5. This can be achieved by the use of the **InputBox()** macro command, which creates a dialogue box and returns the information entered into it. The general format of this macro command is:

```
Variable = InputBox("message")
```

and returns the value typed on the keyboard into the *variable*.

In the macro shown on the next page, we have tried to show the power of Visual Basic without making the example too complicated. First you are asked to give a percentage rate, then the macro calculates the increment and places the value of rate in G5, and stores the original contents of B6:D6 into the three variables, Xjan, Xfeb, and Xmar.

Next, the calculations take place and the results are entered in cell range B6:D6. Finally, a dialogue box is displayed (it can be moved out of the way) asking you to press the **OK** button in order to restore the original contents to the 'Wages' cell range, and changes the contents of G5 to 0 (zero).

Note: This macro only works if the active worksheet is **Sheet1** when you start the macro. If the active sheet is the macro module, then a run time error is encountered.

Finally, save this workbook as **AUTOPRO 4** before attempting to run it.

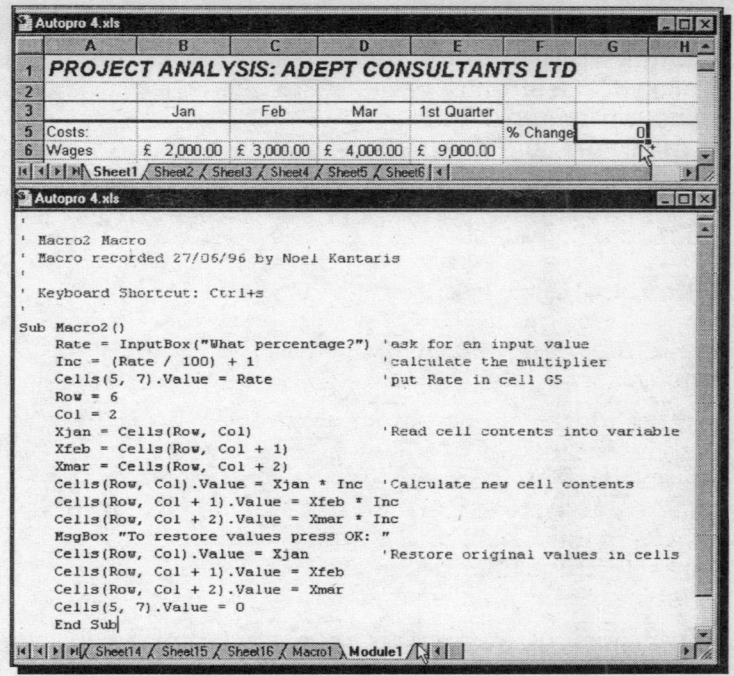

```
Autopro 4.xls                                          _ □ ×

       A         B         C         D         E         F         G         H
 1  PROJECT ANALYSIS: ADEPT CONSULTANTS LTD
 2
 3            Jan       Feb       Mar      1st Quarter
 5  Costs:                                           % Change            0
 6  Wages    £ 2,000.00 £ 3,000.00 £ 4,000.00 £ 9,000.00

  ◄ ► ►│ Sheet1 / Sheet2 / Sheet3 / Sheet4 / Sheet5 / Sheet6 │◄      ►
```

```
Autopro 4.xls                                          _ □ ×

'
'  Macro2 Macro
'  Macro recorded 27/06/96 by Noel Kantaris
'
'  Keyboard Shortcut: Ctrl+s
'
Sub Macro2 ()
    Rate = InputBox("What percentage?")   'ask for an input value
    Inc = (Rate / 100) + 1                'calculate the multiplier
    Cells(5, 7).Value = Rate              'put Rate in cell G5
    Row = 6
    Col = 2
    Xjan = Cells(Row, Col)                'Read cell contents into variable
    Xfeb = Cells(Row, Col + 1)
    Xmar = Cells(Row, Col + 2)
    Cells(Row, Col).Value = Xjan * Inc    'Calculate new cell contents
    Cells(Row, Col + 1).Value = Xfeb * Inc
    Cells(Row, Col + 2).Value = Xmar * Inc
    MsgBox "To restore values press OK: "
    Cells(Row, Col).Value = Xjan          'Restore original values in cells
    Cells(Row, Col + 1).Value = Xfeb
    Cells(Row, Col + 2).Value = Xmar
    Cells(5, 7).Value = 0
    End Sub

  ◄ ◄ ► ►│ Sheet14 / Sheet15 / Sheet16 / Macro1 \ Module1 /│◄     ►
```

Visual Basic has many more statements, commands
and functions which can be used to build and run your
application in special ways. What we have tried to do
here is to introduce you to the subject and give you
some idea of the power of this programming language.
A fuller explanation of Visual Basic is beyond the scope
of this book.

8. OTHER TOOLS AND CAPABILITIES

Apart from the **Spelling** and **AutoCorrect** tools, to be found under the **Tools** menu option, Excel comes with integrated Auditor, and tools to solve what-if type of problems such as the Goal Seek, What-if Tables, Solver and Scenarios. A short description of each of these is given below.

The Auditor

You use the Auditor to analyse the way your worksheet is structured, or for locating the source of errors in formulae.

When you invoke the Auditor by selecting the **Tools, Auditing** command, the options sub-menu is displayed, as shown below.

Trace Precedents
Trace Dependents
Trace Error
Remove All Arrows
Show Auditing Toolbar

In this you can specify what you want to audit on the current file (for a description of the options see below), the default being **Trace Precedents**.

The Audit options have the following functions:

Option	Function
Trace precedents	Identifies all cells in the audit file that provide data for a particular formula.
Trace dependents	Identifies all formulae in the audit file that refer to a particular cell.
Trace Error	Identifies all cells involved in the production of an error, such as a circular reference.

101

Remove All Arrows	Removes the identifying arrows placed on the worksheet as a result of invoking the previous options.
Show Auditing Toolbar	Toggles the display of the Auditing Toolbar on and off.

As an example, we show below an audit on the file **PROJECT 3**, for the first two options.

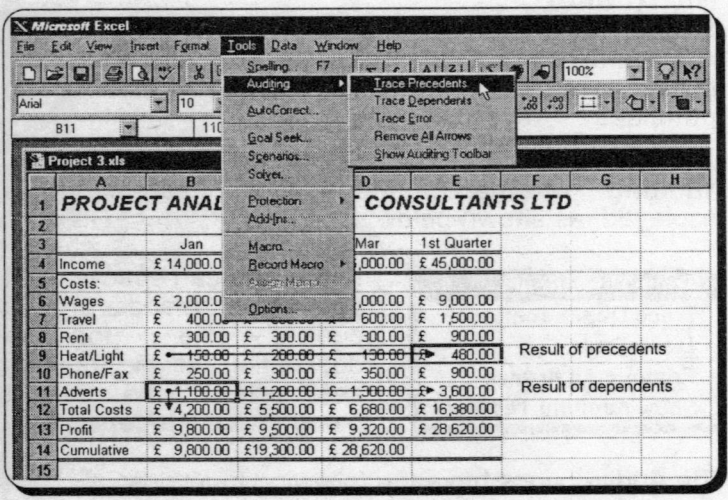

Save this file under the filename **TOOLS 1**, as we will be using it to illustrate the next Excel Tool.

The Goal Seek

You use the **Goal Seek** to fine-tune a formula that gives you the required result by changing one of the variables that affect the final value. As an example, we will use the information in the **TOOLS 1** file. If you don't have this file, use the **PROJECT 3** file and save it as **TOOLS 2**.

To effectively use Goal Seek, you must adhere to the following procedure:

* Type the formula to be fine-tuned by Goal Seek in a cell. We will use the **=sum(B4:D4)** formula in cell E4 of our example.

* Invoke Goal Seek, by using the **Tools, Goal Seek** command which displays the Goal Seek dialogue box shown below.

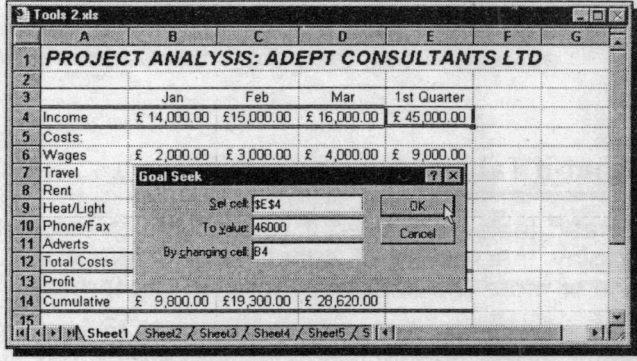

In this dialogue box you can specify in the **Set cell** box the address or range name of the cell that contains the formula you want to fine-tune, as shown above. In the **To value** box you type the value you want the formula in the formula cell to equate to when Goal Seek solves the problem, while in the **By changing cell** box the address of the cell whose value Goal Seek can change.

- Click the **OK** button to find an answer to the problem, displayed below. If it can't be done, you will be told.

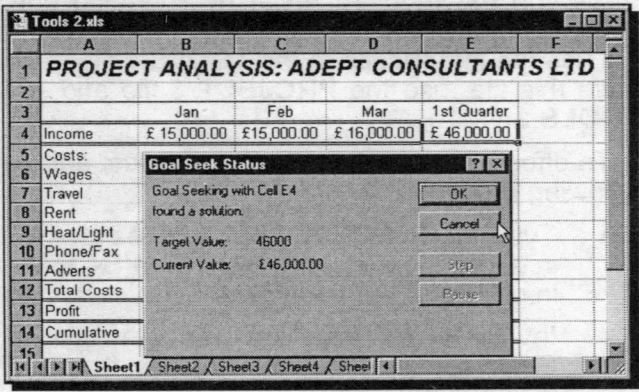

If you don't want to lose the original values in the adjustable cell, then press the **Cancel** button.

What-if Tables

What-if tables are used if you require to calculate and display the results of substituting different values for one or more (up to three) variables in a formula.

For example, suppose we wanted to examine the effect to the quarterly profits of ADEPT Consultants if we varied the quarterly income from £35,000 to £55,000, in steps of £5,000. This problem is, of course, rather trivial, but suppose at the same time we expected a wage award increase of between 0% to 3%, while all other costs were tied to inflation which could change from 3% to 5%. This becomes rather difficult to analyse. However, using what-if tables reduces the problem to something more manageable.

A Two-Input What-if Table:

To illustrate the above problem, but simplifying it by forgetting inflation for the moment, we will use the **TOOLS 1** file (you could use **PROJECT 3** instead). Use the **Window, Freeze Panes** command, then fill in the range F2:K9, as shown below:

	F5	▼	=G3-(E6*(1+G2)+SUM(E7:E11))				

Tools 3.xls

	A	E	F	G	H	I	J	K
1	**PROJECSULTANTS LTD**							
2			Wage incr	0%				
3		1st Quarter	Income	£35,000				
4	Income	£ 45,000.00						
5	Costs:		£18,620	£35,000	£40,000	£45,000	£50,000	£55,000
6	Wages	£ 9,000.00	0%					
7	Travel	£ 1,500.00	1%					
8	Rent	£ 900.00	2%					
9	Heat/Light	£ 480.00	3%					
10	Phone/Fax	£ 900.00						
11	Adverts	£ 3,600.00						
12	Total Costs	£ 16,380.00						
13	Profit	£ 28,620.00						
14	Cumulative							

Sheet1 / Sheet2 / Sheet3 / Sheet4 / Sheet5 / Sheet6 /

Note: A two-input what-if table has two input cells - in our example these are: Input 1 in cell G2 (which refers to the rows) and input 2 in cell G3 (which refers to the columns), representing 'Wage increases' and 'Income', respectively. The value in each of these cells is the first value in their respective ranges, which are F6:F9 and G6:K5. Thus, income varies from £35,000 to £55,000, while wage increases vary from 0% to 3%. Finally, a formula is required in cell F5 which represents profits and which refers to the two input cells defined above. The formula used is:

```
=G3-(E6*(1+G2)+SUM(E7:E11))
```

To verify that this formula is correct, change the input in the 'Income' cell (G3) to £45,000, which should give you the same profit in cell F5 as that shown in cell E13.

The formula in a two-input what-if table must be placed in the top-left corner of the table. Which cell is declared as a 'row input' and a 'column input' in the Table dialogue box is very important. In the case of a one-input what-if table, Excel expects the input range to be either in one column, with the formula placed at the top of the next column to the right of the input column, or in one row, with the formula placed at the top of the next row to the left of the input row.

Before proceeding with the analysis of our problem, save your work under the filename **TOOLS 3**, then select the effective table range F5:K9 by highlighting it. Next, use the **Data, Table** command and enter in the displayed dialogue box the information shown below:

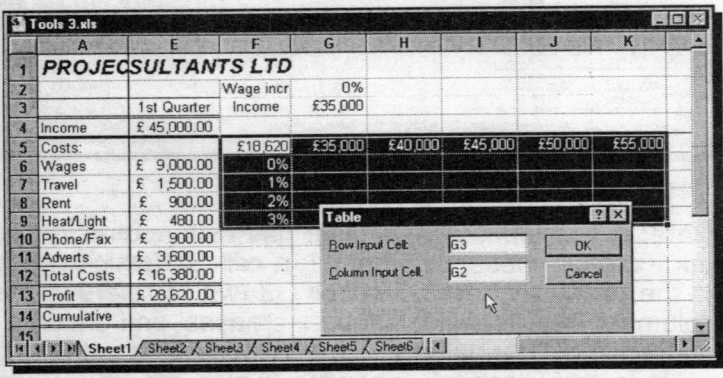

Selecting the **OK** button, displays the results displayed on the next page.

	A	E	F	G	H	I	J	K
1	**PROJECSULTANTS LTD**							
2			Wage incr	0%				
3		1st Quarter	Income	£35,000				
4	Income	£ 45,000.00						
5	Costs:		£18,620	£35,000	£40,000	£45,000	£50,000	£55,000
6	Wages	£ 9,000.00	0%	£18,620	£23,620	£28,620	£33,620	£38,620
7	Travel	£ 1,500.00	1%	£18,530	£23,530	£28,530	£33,530	£38,530
8	Rent	£ 900.00	2%	£18,440	£23,440	£28,440	£33,440	£38,440
9	Heat/Light	£ 480.00	3%	£18,350	£23,350	£28,350	£33,350	£38,350
10	Phone/Fax	£ 900.00						
11	Adverts	£ 3,600.00						
12	Total Costs	£ 16,380.00						
13	Profit	£ 28,620.00						
14	Cumulative							
15								

Sheet1 / Sheet2 / Sheet3 / Sheet4 / Sheet5 / Sheet6

Editing a Data Table:

The input values and formula in the top leftmost column of a data table can be edited at any time. However, the actual results calculated within the data table cannot be edited individually, because they are an array. Some editing operations require you to select the entire data table, while others require you to select only the resulting values. For example:

- To clear the resulting values from a data table, select the resulting values only (G6:G9 in our example) and press the <Del> key. Individual resulting values cannot be cleared separately.

- To copy resulting values from a data table, select them and use the **Edit, Copy** command. Doing this results in copying the values only, not the formulae for those values. Subsequent use of the **Paste Special** command converts the resulting values array into a range of constant values.

- To move, delete, or modify a table, first select the entire data table (F5:K9 in our example). If you are moving the table, having selected it, then click the border of the selection and drag it to a new location on your worksheet.

The Solver

You use the Solver if you want to analyse data in a worksheet and solve 'what-if' type of problems. Solver is ideal for problems that have more than one answer. It can investigate different options and present you with alternative solutions, including the best match to your requirements.

To use Solver, you start with a worksheet model. Solver problems can be set up in one or more worksheet files in memory, by selecting which cells to adjust, adding logical formulae, and defining the limits of the required answers.

As an example, let us analyse more closely ADEPT Consultants' 1st Quarter results. We use the information held in Sheet1 of the **TOOLS 1** file (you could use the **PROJECT 3** file instead). On a Sheet other than Sheet1 of either file, we add the following information:

	A	B	C	D	E	F	G	H
2								
3		Type	Home	Abroad	Total			
4								
5	Number		30	20				
6	Income/consultancy		666.6666	1250				
7	Hours/consultancy		60	160				
8	Costs/consultancy		213.3333	500				
9								
10	Total Income		20000	25000	45000			
11	Total Costs		6400	10000	16400			
12	Total Hours		1800	3200	5000			
13	Total Profit		13600	15000	28600			
14								
15	Constraints							
16	Maximum hours available<=6000							
17	Minimum Home Consultancies >=25							
18	Minimum Abroad Consultancies >=15							
19	Minimum Profit >=28600							
20								

Tools 4.xls — Sheet1 \ **Sheet2** \ Sheet3 \ Sheet4 \ Sheet5

What we assume here is that ADEPT Consultants operate both at home and abroad. In the first quarter they undertook 30 consultancies at home and 20 consultancies abroad.

The range C5:D8 holds numerical information on the income, hours taken, and the costs per consultancy, respectively.

In range C10:D13 we have entered formulae to calculate the total income, costs, hours spent, and profit made from each type of consultancy from information held in range C5:D8, while range E10:E13 summates the two types of consultancies.

Cells E12 and E13 hold the total time spent in consultancies and the total profit made, respectively, which is very important information.

What we would like to do now is to increase the consultancies to make up the maximum available time in the three month period, which is 6000 hours, while maximising the profit. The question is 'what mixture of consultancies (home or abroad) is more profitable given two more constraints'?

Starting the Solver:

To start Solver use the **Tools, Solver** command, which displays the following Solver Parameters dialogue box:

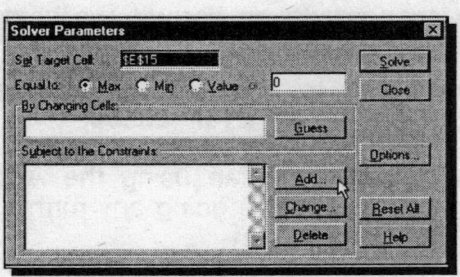

Next, we would like to enter the constraints under which we will impose a solution to our problem. These can be added, changed or deleted with the use of the three buttons at the bottom of the Solver Parameters dialogue box shown above.

Entering Constraints:

At the bottom of the worksheet, we have included certain constraints, discussed below, which are entered as logical formulae in the range E16:E19 using the Add Constraint dialogue box, shown here, by clicking the **Add** button on the Solver Parameters dialogue box.

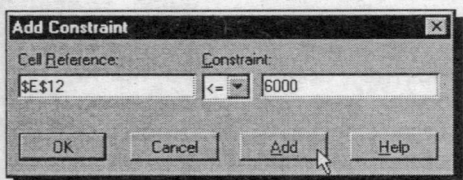

After entering each one of these, press the **Add** button so that you can enter the next one.

The logic behind these constraints is as follows:

- Since the maximum available hours in a quarter must remain less than or equal to 6000 hours, we enter in cell E16 the formula **E12<=6000**.

- Since a long term contract with the government requires that at least 25 consultancies are undertaken at home, we enter in cell E17 the formula **C5>=25**.

- Since a similar long term contract with a foreign government requires that at least 15 consultancies are undertaken abroad, we enter in cell E18 the formula **D5>=15**.

- Since we would like to maximise profits, we enter in cell E19 the formula **E13>=28600**.

After entering these logical formulae using the Add Constraint dialogue box, and before going any further, save your work as **TOOLS 4**.

Solving a Problem:

Once the last constraint is inserted into the Add Constraint dialogue box, pressing the **OK** button causes the return of the Solver Preferences box.

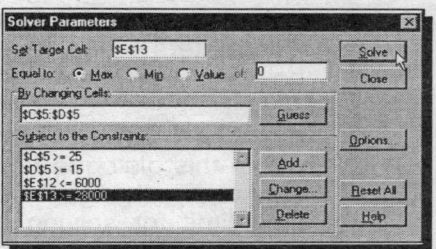

Next, specify the **Set Target Cell**, as shown, then the adjustable cells in the **By Changing Cells** box - these are cells that contain values that Solver can adjust when it searches for an answer, and finally, press the **Solve** button. When Solver finds a solution, it places the answer in the worksheet and displays the Solver Results dialogue box, as shown below.

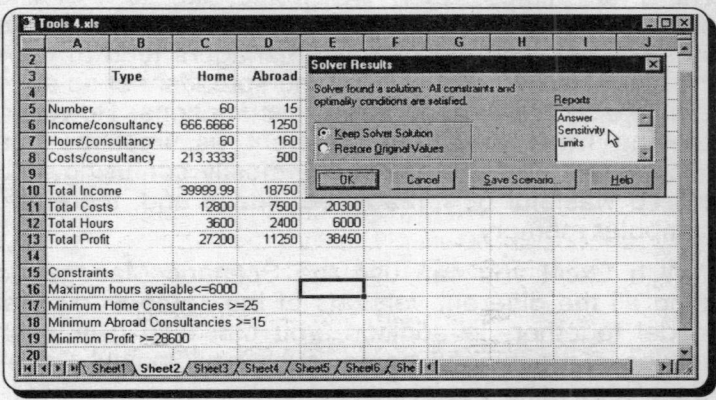

You now have a choice of either keeping the values found by Solver, or reverting to the original worksheet values. Also from the **Reports** section of the dialogue box you can choose to display one of three report types: Answer, Sensitivity, and Limits. Selecting one of these causes Excel to produce an appropriate report and place it in a separate Sheet.

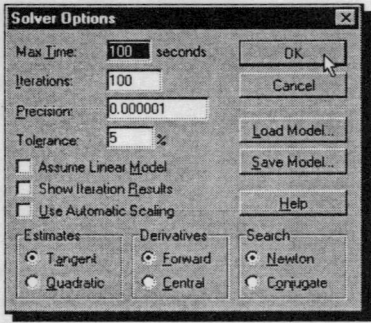

If a problem is too complex for the default settings of Solver, then click at the **Options** button on the Solver Parameters dialogue box to display the Solver Options dialogue box. From within this dialogue box you can change the time limit for solving a problem, the maximum iterations allowed, and even select the type of model to be used.

Managing What-if Scenarios

There are times when we would like to examine different what-if scenarios created from a single spreadsheet model. Normally, managers tend to copy the model to different parts of the spreadsheet so as to examine and display different assumptions. However, keeping track of all the different assumptions can become extremely problematic, mostly confusing, and indeed wasteful of spreadsheet space and, therefore, computer memory.

With Excel you can use the Scenario Manager to keep all the different versions of the same worksheet model together. In addition, you can also give each version a meaningful name, such as 'Original Case', 'Best Case', and 'Worst Case'.

To illustrate the method, we will use the **TOOLS 4** example which we employed when discussing the Solver. In addition, we assume that it is possible to reduce the number of hours it takes ADEPT Consultants to complete a consultancy at home or abroad, but if one is reduced the other is increased by the same amount.

The model looks as follows with '% Changes' added in columns F and G, the contents of cells C7 and D7 changed to =60*(1+F7) and =160*(1+G7), respectively, and the overall profit now also displayed in column H. Save the result as **TOOLS 5**. Since we will be optimising our solutions, you must learn to use Solver first.

	A	B	C	D	E	F	G	H	I
2									
3		Type	Home	Abroad	Total	%	Changes	Profit	
4						Home	Abroad		
5	Number		30	20				£28,600	
6	Income/consultancy		666.6666	1250					
7	Hours/consultancy		60	160		0%	0%		
8	Costs/consultancy		213.3333	500					
9									
10	Total Income		20000	25000	45000				
11	Total Costs		6400	10000	16400				
12	Total Hours		1800	3200	5000				
13	Total Profit		13600	15000	28600				
14									
15	Constraints								
16	Maximum hours available<=6000								
17	Minimum Home Consultancies >=25								
18	Minimum Abroad Consultancies >=15								
19	Minimum Profit >=28600								

Now enter 0% change on the hours per consultancy on both the home and abroad input cells, then run the Solver for an optimum answer on profits using the already defined constraints. This gives us a profit of £38,450, which is in fact our no change scenario.

Next, click the **Save Scenario** button on the Solver Results dialogue box to activate the Scenario Manager which displays the Save Scenario dialogue box, as shown on the next page.

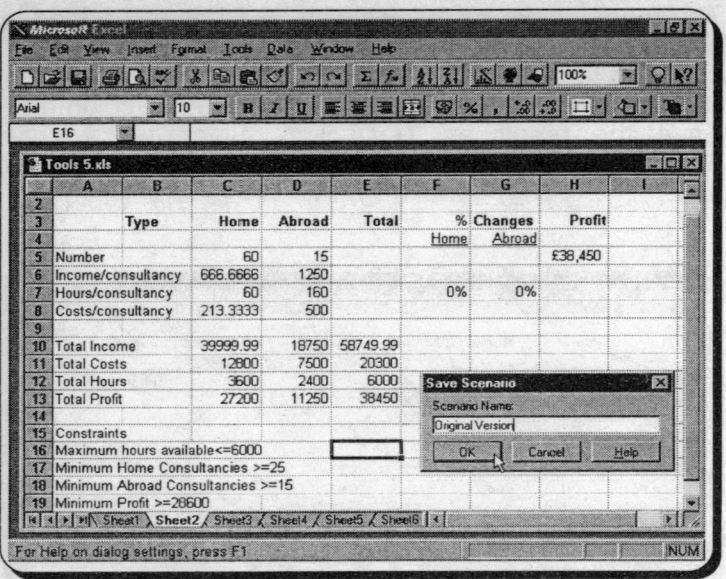

Now add the description 'Original Version' and press the **OK** button, which returns you to the Solver Results dialogue box. Next, press the **OK** button to 'Keep the Solver Solution' then change the contents of cells F7 and G7 to –5% and 5%, respectively, and activate the Solver for an optimum answer on profits, saving the scenario as 'Negative Home Change'.

Finally, change the contents of cells F7 and G7 to 5% and –5%, respectively, and then repeat the above procedure, but saving this version as 'Positive Home Change'.

To see and select any one of the defined scenarios, use the **Tools, Scenarios** command which displays the Scenario Manager dialogue box, shown on the next page, with all the different versions of our solutions listed. To look at the results of one of these, simply highlight it and press the **Show** button.

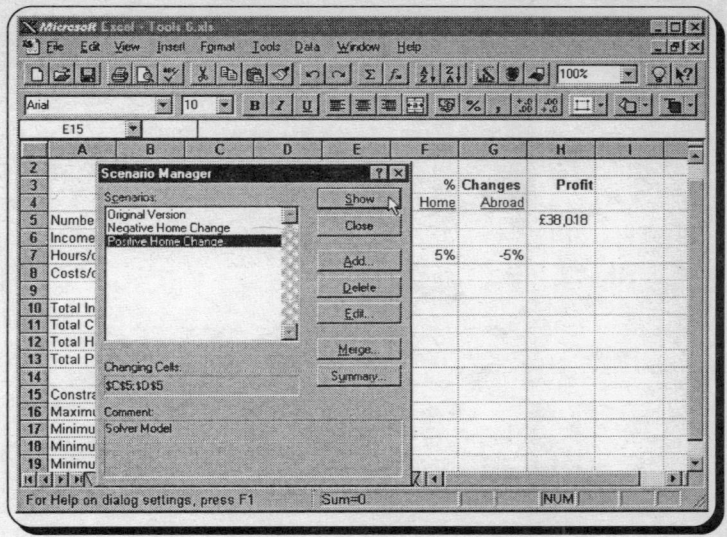

Save the above work as **TOOLS 6**, if you plan to work with it.

Last but not least, Scenario Manager allows you to merge several versions together and define them as a scenario, and create a summary report - you have a choice of two. The first report is a 'scenario summary', while the second is a 'scenario pivot table'. With the pivot table you get an instant what-if analysis of different scenario combinations.

9. SHARING INFORMATION

You can link or embed all or part of an existing file created either in an Office application or in any other application that supports Object Linking and Embedding (OLE). However, if an application does not support OLE, then you must use the copy/cut and paste commands to copy or move information from one application to another.

In general, you copy, move, link or embed information depending on the imposed situation, as follows:

Imposed Situation	Method to Adopt
Inserted information will not need updating, or Application does not support OLE.	Copy or move
Inserted information needs to be automatically updated in the destination file as changes are made to the data in the source file, or Source file will always be available and you want to minimise the size of the destination file, or Source file is to be shared amongst several users.	Link
Inserted information might need to be updated but source file might not be always accessible, or Destination files needs to be edited without having these changes reflected in the source file.	Embed

Copying or Moving Information

To copy or move information between programs running under Windows, such as Microsoft applications, is extremely easy. To move information, use the drag and drop facility, while to copy information, use the **Edit, Copy** and **Edit, Paste** commands.

To illustrate the technique, we will create a file in a word processor (in this case Lotus AmiPro) containing the above sentence, then copy it into **PROJECT 3**. We will consider the following two possibilities:

Source File Available without Application:

We assume that you only have the source file **TESTDOC.SAM** on disc, but not the application that created it (that is you don't have Lotus AmiPro). In such a situation, you can only copy the contents of the whole file to the destination (in our case an Excel worksheet). To achieve this, do the following:

- Start Excel, open **PROJECT 3** and minimise it on the Taskbar.

- Use My Computer (or Explorer) to locate the file whose contents you want to copy into Excel.

- Click the filename that you want to copy, hold the mouse button down and point to Excel on the Taskbar until the application opens.

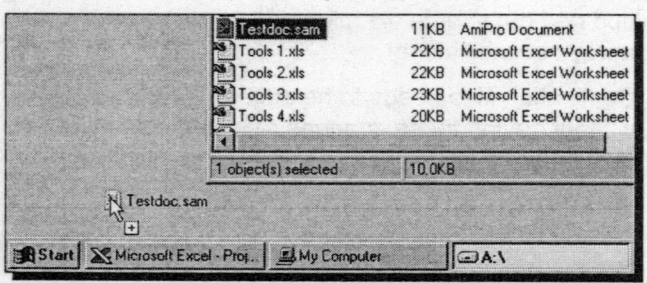

118

- While still holding the mouse button down, move the mouse pointer into Excel's open worksheet to the point where you would like to insert the contents of **TESTDOC.SAM**.

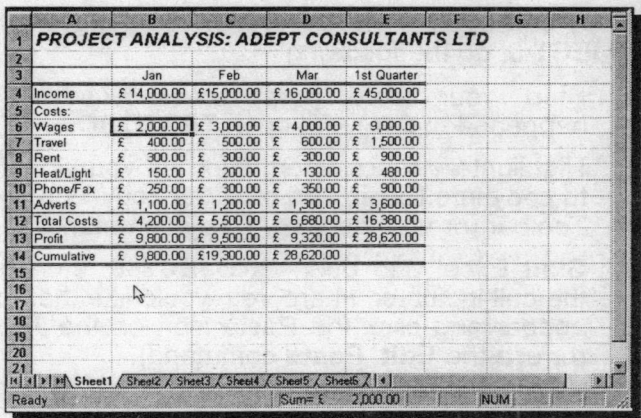

- Release the mouse button to place the contents of **TESTDOC.SAM** into Excel at that point.

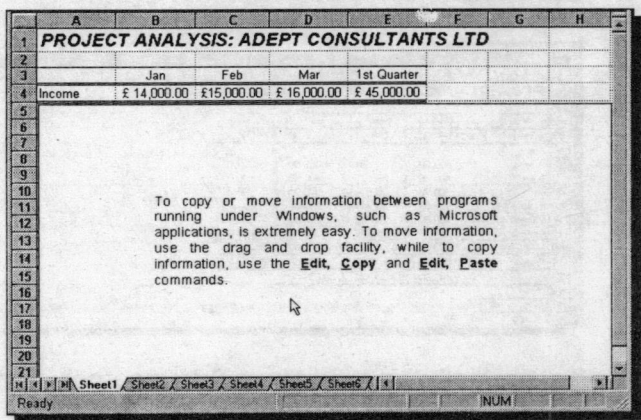

Source File and Application Available:

Assuming that you have both the file and the application that created it on your computer, you can copy all or part of the contents of the source file to the destination file. Here we also consider two possibilities:

To copy part of the **TESTDOC.SAM** into the worksheet **PROJECT 3**, do the following:

- Start your word processor (whichever you happened to use) and open **TESTDOC**.

- Highlight as much information as you would like to copy into Excel, and click the copy icon on the Toolbar (or use the **Edit, Copy** command).

- Start Excel and open **PROJECT 3**, then place the cell indicator where you would like the text to appear and click the Paste icon on the Toolbar (or use the **Edit, Paste** command).

The result is shown below. Note that all the text appears on one cell because there were no hard returns in the original text.

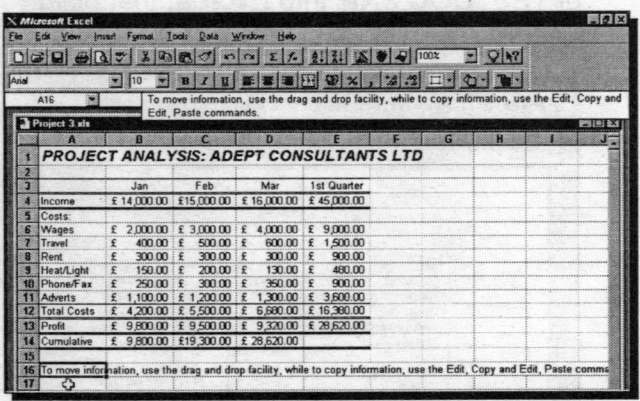

However, normally we tend to want to incorporate parts of a worksheet into a document, not the other way round as shown above.

To copy part of the worksheet **PROJECT 3** into a document, do the following:

- Start Excel and open **PROJECT 3**.

- Highlight as much information as you would like to copy and click the copy icon on the Toolbar (or use the **Edit, Copy** command).

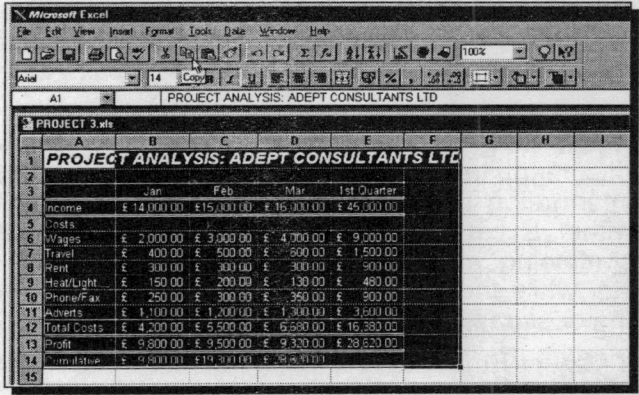

- Start your word processor, place the insertion pointer at the desired place, and click the Paste icon on the Toolbar (or use the **Edit, Paste** command).

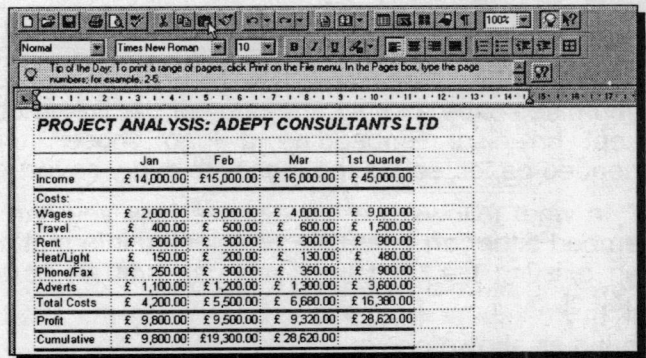

Object Linking and Embedding

Object Linking is copying information from one file (the source file) to another file (the destination file) and maintaining a connection between the two files. When information in the source file is changed, then the information in the destination file is automatically updated. Linked data is stored in the source file, while the file into which you place the data stores only the location of the source and displays a representation of the linked data.

For example, you would use Object Linking if you would want an Excel chart included in, say, a Word document to be updated whenever you changed the information used to create the chart in the first place within Excel. In such a case, the Excel worksheet containing the chart would be referred to as the source file, while the Word document would be referred to as the destination file.

Object Embedding is inserting information created in one file (the source file) into another file (the container file). After such information has been embedded, the object becomes part of the container file. When you double-click an embedded object, it opens in the application in which it was created in the first place. You can then edit it in place, and the original object in the source application remains unchanged.

Thus, the main differences between linking and embedding are where the data is stored and how it is updated after you place it in your file. Linking saves you disc space as only one copy of the linked object is kept on disc. Embedding a logo chosen for your headed paper, saves the logo with every saved letter!

In what follows, we will discuss how you can link or embed either an entire file or selected information from an existing file, and how you can edit an embedded object.

Embedding a New Object:

To embed a new object into an application, do the following:

- Open the container file, say Excel, and click where you want to embed the new object.

- Use the **Insert, Object** command, to open the Object dialogue box, shown below, when the **Create New** tab is clicked.

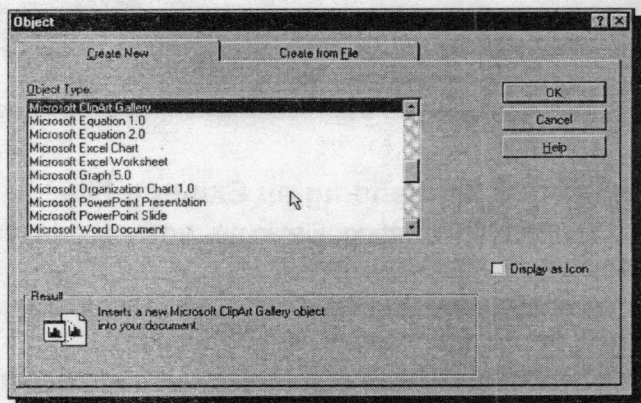

Note that only applications which are installed on your computer and support linking and embedding appear in the **Object Type** box.

- In the **Object Type** box, click the type of object you want to create, and press **OK**.

As an example, we selected Microsoft ClipArt (you could select a different application) which opens the Microsoft ClipArt Gallery from which we selected the

object shown here from the Currency category. Pressing the **Insert** button on the ClipArt application, embeds the object within Excel. Double-clicking on such an object, opens up the original application.

123

If you were able to follow our suggestions, your worksheet should now look as shown below. We saved this worksheet as **SHARE 2**.

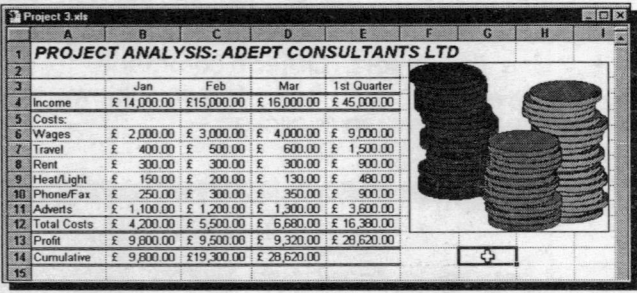

Linking or Embedding an Existing File:

To embed an existing file in its entirety into another application, do the following:

- Open the container file, say Word, and click where you want to embed the file.

- Use the **Insert, Object** command, to open the Object dialogue box, shown below, when the **Create from File** tab is clicked.

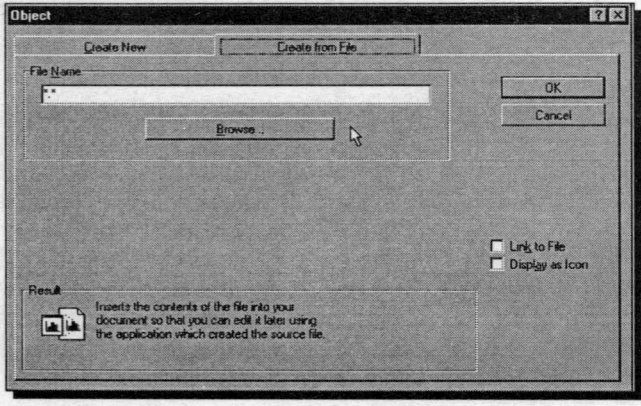

To locate the file you want to link or embed, click **Browse**, and then select the options you want.

- In the **File Name** box, type the name of the file you want to link or embed.

- To maintain a link to the original file, check the **Link to File** box.

Note: To insert graphics files, use the **Insert, Picture** command instead of the **Insert, Object** command. This opens up the Insert Picture dialogue box which allows you to specify within a **Look in** box the folder and file you want to insert.

As an example, we used the **Insert, Object** command while **PROJECT 3** was opened, and selected the **ACCOUNT.WMF** picture file from Microsoft's ClipArt folder. The result is displayed below.

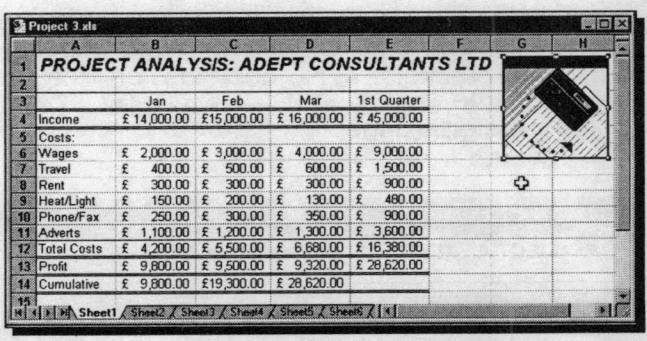

Save this Excel worksheet under the filename **SHARE 3**.

Editing an Embedded Object:

If the application in which you created an embedded object is installed on your computer, double-click the object to open it for editing. Some applications start the original application in a separate window and then open the object for editing, while other applications temporarily replace the menus and toolbars in the current application so that you can edit the embedded object in place, without switching to another window.

If the application in which an embedded object was created is not installed on your computer, convert the object to the file format of an application you do have. For example, if your word processed document contains an embedded Microsoft Works Spreadsheet object and you do not have Works, you can convert the object to an Excel Workbook format and edit it in Excel.

Some embedded objects, such as sound and video clips, when double-clicked start playing their contents, instead of opening an application for editing. To edit one of these objects, select it and use the **Edit, {Wave Sound} Object, Edit** command. What appears within the curly brackets here depends on the selected object; wave sound clip in this case. Doing this, displays the following:

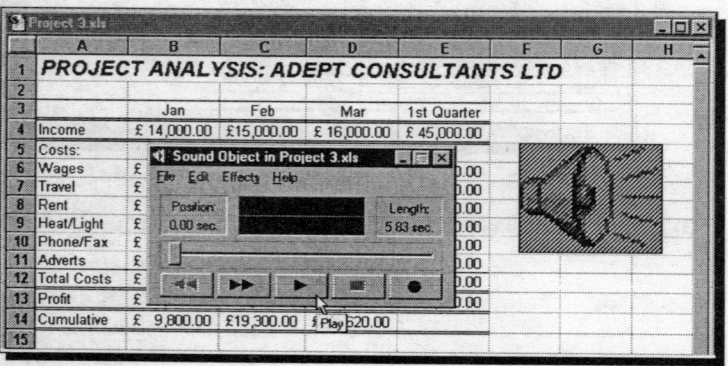

APPENDIX A - FUNCTIONS

Excel's functions are built-in formulae that perform specialised calculations. Their general format is:

name(arg1,arg2,...)

where 'name' is the function name, and 'arg1', 'arg2', etc., are the arguments required for the evaluation of the function. Arguments must appear in a parenthesized list as shown above and their exact number depends on the function being used. However, some functions do not require arguments and are used without parentheses. Examples of these are: FALSE, NA, NOW, PI, RAND, TODAY and TRUE.

There are four types of arguments used with functions: numeric values, range values, string values and conditions, the type used being dependent on the type of function. Numeric value arguments can be entered either directly as numbers, as a cell address, a cell range name or as a formula. Range value arguments can be entered either as a range address or a range name, while string value arguments can be entered as an actual value (a string in double quotes), as a cell address, a cell name, or a formula. Condition arguments normally use logical operators or refer to an address containing a logic formula.

Types of Functions

There are several types of functions in Excel 7, such as mathematical and trigonometric, logical, financial, statistical, text, date and time, information, database, lookup and reference, and commands. Each type requires its own number and type of arguments. These are listed on the next few pages under the various function categories. To find out in detail how these functions can be used, use the Function Wizard, locate the function of interest and press the **Help** button.

Mathematical and Trigonometric Functions:

These functions evaluate a result using numeric arguments. The various functions and what they return are as follows:

Function	Returns
ABS(X)	The absolute value of X.
ACOS(X)	The angle in radians, whose cosine is X (arc cos of X).
ACOSH(X)	The arc (inverse) hyperbolic cosine using the hyperbolic cosine X of an angle.
ASIN(X)	The angle in radians, whose sine is X (arc sin of X).
ASINH(X)	The hyperbolic sine of angle X.
ATAN(X)	The angle in radians, between $\pi/2$ and $-\pi/2$, whose tangent is X (arc tan of X - 2 quadrant).
ATAN2(X,Y)	The angle in radians, between π and $-\pi$, whose tangent is Y/X (arc tan of Y/X - 4 quadrant).
ATANH(X)	The arc (inverse) hyperbolic tangent using the hyperbolic tangent X.
CEILING(N,Sig)	The rounded value of N to nearest integer or nearest multiple of significance.
COMBIN(N,Obj)	The number of combinations N for a given number of objects Obj.
COS(X)	The cosine of X (X in radians).
COSH(X)	The hyperbolic cosine of X.
COUNTBLANK(Rg)	The number of blank cells within range Rg.

COUNTIF(Rg, Cr)	The number of non-blank cells within a range Rg.
DEGREES(X)	The value in degrees in X radians.
EVEN(X)	The rounded value of X away from 0 to the nearest even integer.
EXP(X)	The value of e raised to the power of X.
FACT(X)	The factorial of X.
FLOOR(N, Sig)	A number N down towards zero by nearest multiple of significance Sig.
INT(X)	The integer part of X.
LN(X)	The natural log (base e) of X.
LOG(X,N)	The log of X to a specified base N.
LOG10(X)	The log (base 10) of X.
MDETERM(Ar)	The matrix determinant of an array.
MINVERSE(Ar)	The matrix inverse of an array.
MMULT(Ar1,Ar2)	The matrix product of two arrays.
MOD(X,Y)	The remainder of X/Y.
ODD(X)	The rounded value of X away from 0 to the nearest odd integer.
PI()	The value of π (3.1415926).
POWER(X,N)	The value of X raised to the power of N.
PRODUCT(Ls)	The result of multiplying the values in list Ls.

RADIANS(X)	The value in radians of X degrees.
RAND()	A random number between 0 and 1.
ROMAN(N,Fm)	The Roman format (as text) of number N.
ROUND(X,N)	The value of X rounded to N places.
ROUNDDOWN(X,N)	The rounded value of X down to the nearest multiple of the power of 10 specified by N.
ROUNDUP(X,N)	The rounded value of X up to the nearest multiple of the power of 10 specified by N.
SIGN(X)	The value of 1 if X is a positive, 0 if X is 0, and −1 if X is negative.
SIN(X)	The sine of angle X (X in rads).
SINH(X)	The hyperbolic sine of angle X (X in rads).
SQRT(X)	The square root of X.
SUBTOTAL(Ls)	The subtotal in a list Ls or a database.
SUM(Rg)	The sum of values in range Rg.
SUMIF(Rg,Cr)	The sum in range Rg that meet a given criteria Cr.
SUMPRODUCT(Ar1,Ar2)	The sum of the products of array components.
SUMSQ(N1,N2)	The sum of the squares of the arguments.
SUMX2MY2(Ar1,Ar2)	The sum of the difference of squares of corresponding values in two arrays.

SUMX2PY2(Ar1,Ar2)	The sum of the sum of squares of corresponding values in two arrays.
SUMXMY2(Ar1,Ar2)	The sum of squares of differences of corresponding values in two arrays.
TAN(X)	The tangent of angle X (X in rads).
TANH(X)	The hyperbolic tangent of angle X (X in rads).
TRUNC(X,N)	The truncated value of X to N decimal places.

Logical Functions:

Logical functions produce a value based on the result of a conditional statement, using numeric arguments. The various functions and what they return are as follows:

Function	*Returns*
AND(N1,N2,N3,..)	The logical value 1 (TRUE) if all its arguments are TRUE.
FALSE()	The logical value 0.
IF(Cr,X,Y)	The value X if Cr is TRUE and Y if Cr is FALSE.
NOT(N)	The reverse logic of its argument N.
OR(N1, N2, ..)	The logical value 1 (TRUE) if any argument is TRUE.
TRUE()	The logical value 1.

Financial Functions:

Financial functions evaluate loans, annuities, depreciation and cash flows over a period of time, using numeric arguments. Where an optional parameter [Tp] is given the function will calculate for either an ordinary annuity or an annuity due, depending on the value you specified for type Tp. Percentages should be entered either as a decimal (for example, 0.155) or with a percent sign (for example, 15.5%). The various functions and what they return are as follows:

Function	*Returns*
DB(Ct,Sg,Lf,Pd)	The depreciation allowance of an asset with an initial value of Ct, life Lf, a final salvage value Sg for a specified period Pd, using the declining balance method.
DDB(Ct,Sg,Lf,Pd)	The double-declining depreciation allowance of an asset, with original cost Ct, predicted salvage value Sg, life Lf, and period Pd.
FV(Rt,Tm,Pt)	The future value of a series of equal payments, each of equal amount Pt, earning a periodic interest rate Rt, over a number of payment periods in term Tm.
IPMT(Rt,Pr,Tm,Pv)	The interest payment for a given period Pr (which must be between 1 and Tm) of a total term Tm of a loan with present value Pv at a constant interest rate Rt.
IRR(Rg,Gs)	The internal rate of return of range Rg of cash flows, based on the approximate percentage guess Gs.

132

MIRR(Rg,Fr,Rr)	The modified internal rate of return for a series of cash-flows, in a range Rg, with interest rates, Fr, paid on money used in cash flows and Rr received on reinvested cash flows.
NPER(Rt,Pt,Pv,Fv)	The number of periods required for a series of equal payments Pt, with a present-value Pv, to accumulate a future-value Fv, at a periodic interest rate Rt.
NPV(Rt,Rg)	The net present value of the series of future cash flows in range Rg, discounted at a periodic interest rate Rt.
PMT(Rt,Tm,Pv,Fv)	The payment on a loan with present value Pv, at interest rate Rt, for Tm number of payments and future value Fv.
PPMT(Rt,Pr,Tm,Pv,Fv)	The principal portion of the periodic payment on a loan of present value Pv, at interest rate Rt for payment periods Pr (between 1 and Tm, the number of payment periods in an anuity), leading to a future value Fv.
PV(Rt,Tm,Pt)	The present value of a series of payments, each of amount Pt, discounted at a periodic interest rate Rt, over a number of payment periods in term Tm.
RATE(Tm,Pt,Pv,Fv)	The periodic interest rate necessary for a present value Pv to grow to a future value Fv, over the number of compounding periods in term Tm at Pt payments per period.

SLN(Ct,Sg,Lf)	The straight line depreciation of an asset of cost Ct for one period, given its predicted salvage value Sg, and life Lf.
SYD(Ct,Sg,Lf,Pd)	The sum-of-the-years' digits depreciation of an asset of cost Ct, given its predicted salvage value Sg, life Lf, and period Pd.
VDB(Ct,Sg,Lf,S,E,*d,s*)	The depreciation of an asset of cost Ct, salvage value Sg, life Lf, over a period from start S to end E. Depreciation-factor *d* and switch *s,* are optional. If *s* is 1 it returns declining balance depreciation for life, else straight-line is used after E.

Statistical Functions:

Statistical functions evaluate lists of values using numeric arguments or cell ranges. The various functions and what they return are as follows:

Function	*Returns*
AVEDEV(Ls)	The average of the absolute deviations of values in list Ls.
AVERAGE(Rg)	The average of values in range Rg.
BETADIST(X,Al,Bt,A,B)	The cumulative beta probability density function.
BETAINV(Pb,Al,Bt,A,B)	The inverse of the cumulative beta probability function.
BINOMDIST(Sc,Tr,Pb,Tp)	The cumulative distribution function if Tp is TRUE, else the probability mass function, with Tr independent trials and Sc successes in trials and Pr probability of success per trial.

134

CHIDIST(X,Fr)	The chi-square distribution, evaluated at X and Fr degrees of freedom for the sample.
CHINV(X,Fr)	The inverse of the one-tailed probability of the chi-squared distribution.
CHITEST(Rg1,Rg2)	The chi-square test for independence on the data in range Rg1, or a chi-square test for goodness of fit on the data in ranges Rg1 and Rg2.
CONFIDENCE(Al,Sd,Sz)	The confidence interval for a population mean.
CORREL(Rg1,Rg2)	The correlation coefficient of values in ranges Rg1 and Rg2.
COUNT(Ls)	The number of values in a list.
COUNTA(Rg)	The number of non-blank values in a range Rg.
COVAR(Rg1,Rg2)	The sample covariance of the values in ranges Rg1 and Rg2.
CRITBINOM(Tr,Pb,Al)	The largest integer for which the cumulative binomial distribution is less than or equal to Al, with Tr Bernoulli trials and a probability of success for a single Bernoulli trial Pb.
DEVSQ(Ls)	The sum of squared deviations of the values in list Ls, from their mean.
EXPONDIST(X,Lm,Ds)	The exponential distribution.
FDIST(X,Fr1,Fr2)	The F-distribution at value X with Fr1 and Fr2 degrees of freedom for the first and second samples.

FINV(Pb,Fr1,Fr2)	The inverse of the F probability distribution.
FISHER(X)	The Fisher transformation.
FISHERINV(Y)	The inverse of the Fisher transformation.
FORECAST(X,Yo,Xo)	The value along a linear trend.
FREQUENCY(Rg,Bin)	The frequency distribution as a vertical array Bin.
FTEST(Rg1,Rg2)	The associated probability of an F-test on data in ranges Rg1 and Rg2. Used to determine if two samples have different variances.
GAMMADIST(X,Al,Bt,Cm)	The gamma distribution.
GAMMAINV(Pb,Al,Bt)	The inverse of the gamma cumulative distribution.
GAMMALN(X)	The natural logarithm of the gamma function.
GEOMEAN(Ls)	Returns the geometric mean of the values in list Ls.
GROWTH(Yo,Xo,Xn,Ct)	The values along an exponential trend.
HARMEAN(Ls)	The harmonic mean of the values in list Ls.
HYPGEOMDIST(Ns,Ssiz,Pp,Psiz)	
	The hypergeometric distribution probability of a given number of successes Ns, given the sample size Ssiz, population success Pp and population size Psiz.
INTERCEPT(Yo,Xo)	The intercept of the linear regression line.

KURT(Rg)	The kurtosis of the values in range Rg.
LARGE(Arr,K)	The largest value in a data set.
LINEST(Yo,Xo,Ct,St)	The parameters of a linear trend.
LOGEST(Yo,Xo,Ct,St)	The parameters of an exponential trend.
LOGINV(Pb,Mn,Sd)	The inverse of the lognormal distribution with parameters mean Mn and standard deviation Sd.

LOGNORMDIST(X,Mn,Sd)

The cumulative lognormal distribution with parameters mean Mn and standard deviation Sd.

MAX(Rg)	The maximum value in a range.
MEDIAN(Ls)	The median value in list Ls.
MIN(Rg)	The minimum value in a range.
MODE(Ls)	The most common value in a data set.

NEGBINOMDIST(Nf,Ns,Pb)

The negative binomial distribution that there will be a number of failures Nf before the number of successes Ns, when the constant probability of success is Pb.

NORMDIST(X,Mn,Sd)	The normal cumulative distribution function for X, with a distribution mean Mn and optional standard deviation Sd.
NORMINV(Pb,Mn,Sd)	The inverse of the normal cumulative distribution.

NORMSDIST(X)	The standard normal cumulative distribution.
NORMSINV(Pb)	The inverse of the standard normal cumulative distribution.
PEARSON(Ar1,Ar2)	The Pearson product moment correlation coefficient.
PERCENTILE(Rg,K)	The Kth sample percentile among the values in range Rg.
PERCENTRANK(Ar,X,Sg)	The percentage rank of a value in a data set.
PERMUT(N,Nc)	The number of ordered sequences (permutations) of Nc chosen objects that can be selected from a total of N objects.
POISSON(X,Mn,Cm)	The Poisson distribution (depending on cumulative factor Cm) of X observed events and Mn expected number of events.
PROB(Rgx,Pb,Ll,Ul)	The probability that values in Rgx range are within lower limit Ll and upper limit Ul of probability Pb.
QUARTILE(Ar,Qrt)	The quartile of a data set.
RANK(It,Rg,Od)	The relative size or position of a value It in a range Rg, relative to other values in the range, ranked in order Od.
RSQ(Yo,Xo)	The square of the Pearson product moment correlation coefficient.
SKEW(Rg)	The skewness of the values in range Rg.
SLOPE(Yo,Xo)	The slope of the linear regression line.

SMALL(Ar,K)	The Kth smallest value in a data set.
STANDARDIZE(X,Mn,Sd)	The normalised value of X from a distribution characterised by mean Mn and standard deviation Sd.
STDEV(Rg)	The population standard deviation of values in range Rg.
STDEVP(Rg)	The standard deviation based on the entire population.
STEYX(Yo,Xo)	The standard error of the predicted y-value for each X in the regression.
TDIST(X,Fr,Tr)	The Student's t-distribution, evaluated at X and Fr degrees of freedom for the sample, with test direction Tr.
TINV(Pb,Fr)	The inverse of the Student's t-distribution.
TREND(Xo,Yo,Xn,Cn)	The values along a linear trend.
TRIMMEAN(Ar,Pb)	The mean of the interior of a data set.
TTEST(Rg1,Rg2,Tl,Tp)	The probability associated with a Student's t-test.
VAR(Rg)	The sample variance of values in range Rg.
VARP(Rg)	The variance of values in range Rg based on entire population.
WEIBULL(X,Al,Bt,Cm)	The Weibull distribution.
ZTEST(Arr,X,Sg)	Returns the two-tailed P-value of a z-test.

Text Functions:

String functions operate on strings and produce numeric or string values dependent on the function.

Function	Returns
CHAR(X)	The character that corresponds to the code number X.
CLEAN(Sg)	The specified string having removed all non-printable characters from it.
CODE(Sg)	The code number for the first character in string Sg.
CONCATENATE(Sg1,Sg2)	One string made up of several strings.
DOLLAR(N,Dm)	A number in text form, using currency format.
EXACT(Sg1,Sg2)	The value 1 (TRUE) if strings Sg1 and Sg2 are exactly alike, otherwise 0 (FALSE).
FIND(Ss,Sg,Sn)	The position at which the first occurrence of search string Ss begins in string Sg, starting the search from search number Sn.
FIXED(N,Dm,Nc)	A number N formatted as text with a fixed number of decimals Dm. Nc is a logical value and if TRUE prevents the inclusion of commas.
LEFT(Sg,N)	The first (leftmost) N characters in string Sg.
LEN(Sg)	The number of characters in string Sg.

LOWER(Sg)	A string with all the letters in Sg converted to lowercase.
MID(Sg,Sn,N)	The N characters from string Sg beginning with the character at Sn.
PROPER(Sg)	A string with all words in string Sg changed to first letter in uppercase and the rest in lowercase.
REPLACE(O,S,N,Ns)	A string with N characters removed from original string O, starting at character S and then inserts new string Ns in the vacated place.
REPT(Sg,N)	A repeated string Sg, N times. Unlike the repeating character (\), the output is not limited by the column width.
RIGHT(Sg,N)	The last (rightmost) N characters in string Sg.
SEARCH(Sg1,O,S)	String Sg1 in original string O, starting at character S.
SUBSTITUTE(Sg,O,Ns,N)	A new string Ns substituted for old string O in a string Sg. N specifies which occurrence of the old text you want to replace.
T(X)	A value X converted into text.
TEXT(X,Fm)	A number X formatted into text.
TRIM(Sg)	A string Sg with no leading, trailing or consecutive spaces.
UPPER(Sg)	All letters in string Sg converted to uppercase.
VALUE(Sg)	The numeric value of string Sg.

Date and Time Functions:

These generate and use serial numbers with dates having integer serial numbers between 1 and 65380 to represent dates between 1 January, 1900 and 31 December 2078, and time having decimal serial numbers starting with 0.000 at midnight and ending with 0.99999 next midnight. The various functions are:

Function	*Returns*
DATE(Yr,Mh,Dy)	The date number of argument Yr,Mh,Dy.
DATEVALUE(Ts)	The number of days from 1 January 1900 of date string Ts.
DAY(Dn)	The day of the month number (1-31) of date number Dn.
DAYS360(Sn,En)	The number of days between Sn and En, based on a year of 12 months, each of 30 days.
HOUR(Tn)	The hour number (0-23) of time number Tn.
MINUTE(Tn)	The minute number (0-59).
MONTH(Dn)	The month number (1-12).
NOW()	The serial number for the current date and time.
SECOND(Tn)	The second number (0-59).
TIME(Hr,Ms,Ss)	The time number of argument Hr,Ms,Ss.
TIMEVALUE(Ts)	The time number of string Ts.
TODAY()	The current date number.
WEEKDAY(Dn)	The day of the week from date number Dn in integer form; 0 (Monday) through 6 (Sunday).
YEAR(Dn)	Returns the year number (0-199) of date number Dn.

Information Functions:

Information functions perform a variety of advanced tasks, such as looking up values in a table, returning information about cells, ranges or the Excel environment. The various functions and what they return are as follows:

Function	Returns
CELL(At,Rg)	Returns the code representing the attribute At of range Rg.
ERROR.TYPE(X)	The error value.
INFO(At)	Returns system information based on the attribute At.
ISBLANK(X)	The value 1 (TRUE), if true.
ISERR(X)	1 (TRUE), if X is an error value except #N/A.
ISERROR(X)	1 (TRUE), if X is any error.
ISLOGICAL(X)	1 (TRUE), if X is a logical value.
ISNA(X)	1 (TRUE), if X contains #N/A.
ISNONTEXT(X)	1 (TRUE), if X is not text.
ISNUMBER(X)	1 (TRUE), if X contains a numeric value.
ISREF(X)	1(TRUE), if X is a reference.
ISTEXT(X)	1 (TRUE), if X is text.
N(X)	A value converted to a number
NA()	The error value #N/A.
TYPE(X)	A number indicating the data type value of X.

Lookup and Reference Functions:

The group of function return values specified by a range reference or array reference. The various functions available and what they return are as follows:

Function	*Returns*
ADDRESS(Rn,Cn)	The cell address specified by row Rn and column Cn.
AREAS(Rf1,Rf2,..)	The number of areas in the list of references.
CHOOSE(K,V0,..,Vn)	The Kth value in the list V0,..,Vn.
COLUMN(Rf)	The column number of a reference.
COLUMNS(Rg)	The number of columns in the range Rg.
HLOOKUP(X,Ar,Rn)	The value of indicated cell by performing a horizontal array look-up by comparing the value X to each cell in the top index row in array Ar, then moves down the column in which a match is found by the specified row number Rn.
INDEX(Rg,Rn,Cn)	The value of the cell in range Rg at the intersection of row-offset Rn, and column-offset Cn.
INDIRECT(Rf)	The cell reference specified in reference Rf in A1-style.
LOOKUP(Lv,Vr,Rv)	The value in a result vector Rv by looking up a value Lv in a vector Nr and moving to the corresponding position in the vector Rv.

LOOKUP(Lv,Ar)	The value in an array cell by looking in the first row or column of an array Ar for the specified lookup value Lv and moving down or across to the last cell.
MATCH(Lv,Ar,Mtc)	The relative position of an element in an array Ar that matches the specified value Mtc of a lookup value Lv.
OFFSET(Rf,Rn,C,Ht,Wh)	A reference of a specified height Ht and width Wh offset from another reference Rf by a specified number of rows Rn and columns Cn.
ROW(Rf)	The row number of a reference.
ROWS(Rg)	The number of rows in a range.
TRANSPOSE(Ar)	The transpose of an array.
VLOOKUP(X,Ar,Cn)	The value of indicated cell by performing a vertical table lookup by comparing the value X to each cell in the first index column, in array Ar, then moves across the row in which a match is found by the specified column number Cn.

Database Functions:

Database functions perform calculations on a database. The database, called the input range, consists of records, which include fields and field names, like Fd below. A criterion range must be set up to select the records from the database that each function uses. The various functions and what they return are as follows:

Function	*Returns*
DAVERAGE(Db,Fd,Cr)	The average of the values in the field Fd that meet the criteria Cr in a database Db.
DCOUNT(Db,Fd,Cr)	The number of non-blank cells in the field Fd that meet the criteria Cr in a database Db.
DCOUNTA(Db,Fd,Cr)	Counts nonblank cells from a specified database and criteria.
DGET(Db,Fd,Cr)	The single value in the field Fd that meet the criteria Cr in a database Db.
DMAX(Db,Fd,Cr)	The maximum value in the field Fd that meet the criteria Cr in a database Db.
DMIN(Db,Fd,Cr)	The minimum value in the field Fd that meet the criteria Cr in a database Db.
DPRODUCT(Db,Fd,Cr)	The result of the product of the values in the field Fd that meet the criteria Cr in a database Db.
DSTDEV(Db,Fd,Cr)	The standard deviation based on the values in the field Fd that meet the criteria Cr in a database Db.

DSTDEVP(Db,Fd,Cr)	The standard deviation based on the entire population of the values in the field Fd that meet the criteria Cr in a database Db.
DSUM(Db,Fd,Cr)	The sum of the values in the field Fd that meet the criteria Cr in a database Db.
DVAR(Db,Fd,Cr)	The estimated variance based on the values in the field Fd that meet the criteria Cr in a database Db.
DVARP(Db,Fd,Cr)	The variance based on the entire population of the values in the field Fd that meet the criteria Cr in a database Db.

INDEX

NOTES

NOTES

COMPANION DISCS TO BOOKS

COMPANION DISCS are available for most books written by the same author(s) and published by BERNARD BABANI (publishing) LTD, as listed at the front of this book (except for those marked with an asterisk). These books contain many pages of file/program listings. There is no reason why you should spend hours typing them into your computer, unless you wish to do so, or need the practice.

COMPANION DISCS come in 3½" format with all example listings.

ORDERING INSTRUCTIONS

To obtain your copy of a companion disc, fill in the order form below or a copy of it, enclose a cheque (payable to **P.R.M. Oliver**) or a postal order, and send it to the address below. Make sure you fill in your name and address and specify the book number and title in your order.

Book No.	Book Name	Unit Price	Total Price
BP		£3.50	
BP		£3.50	
BP		£3.50	
Name		Sub-total	£.............
Address:		P & P (@ 45p/disc)	£.............
		Total Due	£.............

Send to: P.R.M. Oliver, CSM, Pool, Redruth, Cornwall, TR15 3SE

PLEASE NOTE

The author(s) are fully responsible for providing this Companion Disc service. The publishers of this book accept no responsibility for the supply, quality, or magnetic contents of the disc, or in respect of any damage, or injury that might be suffered or caused by its use.